A STRATEGY FOR PEACE

A STRATEGY FOR PEACE

Reflections
of a
Christian Pacifist

by
Frank H. Epp

William B. Eerdmans Publishing Company
Grand Rapids, Michigan

Library of Congress Cataloging in Publication Data

Epp, Frank H   1929-
    A strategy for peace.

    CONTENTS: Sometimes I pray for nuclear war.—
On being afraid of communism.—Evangelism and
peace. [etc.]
    1. Peace (Theology)   I. Title.
II. Title: Reflections of a Christian pacifist.
BT736.4.E66   261.8'73   73-2290
ISBN 0-8028-1516-2

Acknowledgments

"The Unilateral Disarmament of the Church." From *Peacemakers in
a Broken World,* edited by John A. Lapp. Copyright © 1969 by
Herald Press, Scottdale, Pennsylvania 15683. Used by permission.

"Peace Witness as Evangelism." From *Probe,* edited by James Fair-
field. Copyright © 1972 by Herald Press, Scottdale, Pennsylvania
15683. Used by permission.

"American Causes of World War III." From *The Star-Spangled
Beaver: Twenty-Four Canadians Look South,* edited by John H.
Redekop. © 1971 Peter Martin Associates Limited, Toronto, Ontar-
io, Canada MSA 1R7. Used by permission.

To Helen, my wife,
and Marianne, Esther, Marlene,
our daughters

Preface

The peace movement of the 1960s, like that of the 1930s, faded quickly—much too quickly, for its task was not yet completed. The causes of war had not yet been eliminated. The instruments of war had not yet been reduced. And, worst of all, war itself was still raging.

One of several causes for the apparently early demise of the peace movement lay in its lack of depth, the kind of depth a profound religion could have given to it. This lack was not so much its own fault as it was the fault of religion. If much of the peace movement lacked religion, it was also true that religion itself lacked peace. And of the two lacks, the latter was the more serious, for a society's religion, good or bad, strong or weak, eventually translates itself into social policy. A nation whose religions are weak on peace easily becomes a nation religiously preoccupied with war.

It is not that religious spokesmen did not lead out in the movement. They did, and there is good evidence that concerned people of the Christian and Jewish faiths inspired and often led the forces for peace. But the energy of the few was somehow not sufficient to stop the war machine. That machine would have ground to a halt long ago if so much of Christianity had not translated itself into an American chauvinism, if the carrying of the Christian cross of suffering and peace had not been exchanged for waving the national flag of an aggressive materialism and war.

Be that as it may, these essays try to bring the peace movement and North American religion together. It is my thesis that unless the totality of that religion changes, the politics of war will not change nor will the war budgets significantly decrease.

Christian churches have often sought to bring religious renewal to the North American continent, most recently under the banner of Key '73. Elaborate strategy is devised, many of its pages taken straight out of the high pressure sales culture. But the foremost requirement for renewal is not smoother strategy, but purer, more righteous theology. A theology of peace. A better theology is itself a better strategy. In other words, a theology of peace, which gives religion a new content, becomes itself a new strategy for peace.

This, then, is an appeal to those who believe in a kingdom greater than America or Canada, in a king greater than presidents or prime ministers, and in a law higher than the law of the land. It is a challenge to them to go about the business of peace, first in the halls of institutional religion, then on the hills of establishment politics, and along the way, of course, on the highways and byways where the people live and where we will probably first see the signs of the coming kingdom.

The American publisher of this Canadian manuscript has properly asked why the author sometimes speaks as a Canadian, sometimes as an American, sometimes as a North American. The answer is simple. This is how most of us Canadians live. We are citizens of an independent country, which is also a province of the empire, not always an unhappy province. This is true especially of people like me. I have spent some of the best years of my educational life in American schools; some of my most receptive audiences have been on American college campuses. We Canadians know that many decisions affecting our lives are made in Washington as well as Ottawa, and we realize that, for better or for worse, a certain common destiny has already been decided for our continent. As John F. Kennedy said, "Geography has made us neighbors. History has made us friends."

No effort has been made, therefore, to clear up the confusion concerning the national base from which I speak. Underneath or above it all is, I hope, the vision of the coming of the kingdom of God, a warless world, in which justice dwells for all mankind.

Among those to whom I owe much in the preparation of these essays are the people of the Mennonite Central Committee Peace Section, Akron, Pennsylvania, my part-time employers for four beautiful years, as together we strove for peace in Indochina and the Middle East. I am indebted also to the people of the Ottawa Mennonite Church in Canada's capital, where during those same years many of the ideas of these essays were tested. And I must thank my family of four girls, my secretaries, research assistants, filing clerks, and kindest critics, to whom I affectionately dedicate this collection.

Frank H. Epp

Conrad Grebel College
Waterloo, Ontario, Canada
July 1, 1973

Notations
on Context

Most of these essays, first delivered as speeches in the late 1960s and early 1970s, were prepared for college audiences in the USA and Canada (1, 2, 6, 7, 9). The others may be understood in terms of a more specific context. Two come from congresses on evangelism—one Canadian and ecumenical (4), the other Mennonite (3). Number (5) is from a Sunday worship and dialogue with the Hon. John N. Turner, then Minister of Justice and Attorney-General in Canada. A peace teach-in in dialogue with the Hon. Walter Dinsdale, Canadian Member of Parliament, was the occasion for (8). A response to Billy Graham's "Honor America Day," July 4, 1970, in Washington is number (10). Number (11) is the prelude to a 1969 dialogue in Ottawa between Christian militarists from a Canadian Forces Base and Christian pacifists.

Contents

I

Sometimes I Pray for Nuclear War, But I've Never Said Amen!

"O Lord, our God, help us to tear their soldiers in bloody shreds with our shells; . . . help us to drown the thunder of the guns with the shrieks of their wounded, writhing in pain; help us to lay waste their humble homes with a hurricane of fire. . . ."
—Mark Twain

Though I have never yet said Amen, I have sometimes prayed for nuclear war. As terrible as this may sound, you probably have too. In almost every international conflict and war the religions of the countries involved have taken on the form of tribal cults whose priests and adherents offer prayers to God for a nationalistic triumph.

The priests of Canadian tribal Christianity did it in World War I, and the *Canadian Annual Review* is full of clerical support for the war, which was fought "to make the world safe for democracy," but instead opened the floodgates for dictatorships of the left and of the right. In the words of a Canadian Church of England Bishop:

> It is our duty to pray for victory, and to work for it and to fight for it, because we believe that the things for which we are fighting are the things which God would have prevail upon the earth.[1]

The priests of American tribal religion joined them in 1917 and again in 1941. At Pearl Harbor Chaplain Howell M.

Forgy spoke his famous prayer, "Praise the Lord and pass the ammunition," and after the prayer had been set to music, not only did the nation's chaplain-priests have a prayer but American folk religion had a hymn.

Since there are at least two sides to any war, with numerous parties seeking their own ends, it should not surprise us that rather strange and contradictory prayers come before the Lord. Edmund Fuller says that during World War II a French film actor arriving in New York was asked how the French, who had been defeated in the first round, felt about the British, who were still fighting for themselves and for France against the Germans. He said:

> We are both pro-British and anti-British. Those who are pro-British say each night in their prayers, "Please God, let the gallant British win quickly." Those who are anti-British say each night in their prayers, "Please God, let the dirty British win right away."[2]

Mark Twain illustrated the multidimensional aspect of our war prayers in another way. *The War Prayer*, written in 1904 but not published until after Twain's death, illustrates the hypocrisy that causes Christian priests to speak coldly murderous prayers to their God, who has in reality been reduced to a tribal god. Twain points out that a war prayer does not consist only of the spoken word but also of the unspoken feeling, and not only spoken thoughts and feelings, but those thoughts and feelings carried through to their logical conclusion.

The parable begins on Sunday in the church, where veterans and new recruits, all in uniform, are present with their proud parents, wives, sweethearts, brothers, and sisters. The minister reads a war chapter from the Old Testament, which is followed by an organ burst loud enough to shake the building. Then the entire congregation, with glowing eyes and beating hearts, pours forth the tremendous invocation:

> *God the all-terrible! Thou who ordainest,*
> *Thunder thy clarion and lightning thy sword!*

The minister offers a long prayer for "our noble young soldiers ... and their patriotic work," beseeching God to help them "crush the foe" and bring "to their flag and country imperishable honor and glory." He finishes with the fervent appeal: "Bless our arms, grant us victory, O Lord our God, Father and Protector of our land and flag!" At that point an old stranger walks up the aisle noiselessly, his eyes fixed on the minister. As he reaches the altar, he motions the minister to step aside and tells the congregation he has been sent by almighty God to bring a message. He then proceeds to speak a second prayer, which he says is the real, though unspoken, meaning of the first. God has commanded him to put the unuttered feeling, the prayer carried through to its logical conclusion, into words, as follows:

> O Lord our Father, our young patriots, idols of our hearts, go forth to battle—be Thou near them! With them—in spirit—we also go forth from the sweet peace of our beloved firesides to smite the foe. O Lord our God, help us tear their soldiers to bloody shreds with our shells; help us to cover their smiling fields with the pale forms of their patriot dead; help us to drown the thunder of the guns with the shrieks of their wounded, writhing in pain; help us to lay waste their humble homes with a hurricane of fire; help us to wring the hearts of their unoffending widows with unavailing grief; help us to turn them out roofless with their little children to wander unfriended the wastes of their desolated land in rags and hunger and thirst, sports of the sun flames of summer and the icy winds of winter, broken in spirit, worn with travail, imploring Thee for the refuge of the grave and denied it—for our sakes who adore Thee, Lord, blast their hopes, blight their lives, protract their bitter pilgrimage, make heavy their steps, water their war with their tears, stain the white snow with the blood of their wounded feet! We ask it, in the spirit of love, of Him who is the Source of love, and who is the ever-faithful refuge and friend of all that are sore beset and seek His aid with humble and contrite hearts. Amen.[3]

"Ye have prayed it," the man concludes, as he leaves the altar. The people only shake their heads, saying that the man is a lunatic, because there is no sense in what he has said. Yet, Mark Twain was convinced that the prayer parable was so loaded that, courageous as he was, he withheld publication in his lifetime.

If all our desires and aspirations as revealed by our deeds

are prayers, and they are, and if these desires and aspirations followed through to their logical conclusions are prayers, and they are, then there has been considerable praying for nuclear war in the thirty-odd years since the first self-supporting nuclear reaction at the University of Chicago in December 1942. I have sometimes prayed for nuclear war, though I have never said Amen, and I should like to explain how, why, and when.

* * *

To begin with, the boy in me has prayed, for he likes nothing better than a big bang.

The boy recalls with joy the firecracker explosions of July 1 (July 4 in the USA), the clap of thunder on stormy summer nights on the prairies, the blasting of Douglas fir stumps on the west coast, and the cannon salutes to greet royalty. To the extent that the boy lives on, he has wondered what it might be like to have Russia's billions of tons of TNT in nuclear explosives meet the billions of tons of TNT of the American military system. What a bang that would be!

The thought is a continuation of the Mother Goose poem about all the seas being one sea, all the trees being one tree, all the axes being one axe, and all the men being one man, and the great man taking the great axe to chop down the great tree to let it fall into the great sea, to see what a splash-bang that would be? Rewritten in today's language that poem might read something like this:

> *If all the presidents were one president,*
> *What a big president that would be!*
> *And if all his fingers would be one finger,*
> *What a big finger that would be!*
> *And if all the bombs were one bomb,*
> *What a big bomb that would be!*
> *And if all the missiles were one missile,*
> *What a big missile that would be!*
> *And if all the buttons were one button,*
> *What a big button that would be!*
> *And if all the Communists were one Communist,*
> *What a fine target that would be!*
> *And if the big president lifted his big finger*
> *And placed it on the big button*

So as to activate the big missile carrying the big bomb
So that it would directly hit the Communist
What a big bang that would be!

I have it on good authority that it would be the last bang most of us would ever hear, and that is why I've never said Amen. Besides, Paul said that as a man grew up he should put away childish things, such as playing with bombs. He implied that a man should get as much excitement out of the quiet and peaceful bursts of life-giving energy from atomic power plants as from the bangs of atomic warheads.

But some boys never grow up. Unless they can bomb, life has no purpose and meaning for them. Or why is it that the U.S. Air Force and the Pentagon, in selling their activities to the American people, reported with such regularity the tonnage dropped on little Vietnam as compared to Europe and World War II? Is it perhaps that the Pentagon and the people *need* bigger and bigger bangs? Could this need not set off nuclear war?

*   *   *

Second, the zealot in me has prayed, for he likes few things better than to let people know where he stands.

"Bomb them back into the stone age" if they do not knuckle under, said a general who once ran for the vice presidency of the United States. And why not? Why can't I suggest a few bombs, just to let the world know where I stand if Jesus' loyal disciples could ask for fire from heaven to teach stubborn Palestinian villagers a lesson? if God's "chosen people" can drop bombs on refugee camps just to put Arabs in their place for having such a silly notion as wanting to return to their homeland? if America's foremost evangelist, speaking at a presidential prayer breakfast, can recommend a fire-bringing and sword-wielding Christ at the very time that the president is escalating his napalm drops?

As a zealot I find myself in very good company. But I have never said Amen, because the words of the fire-bringing Christ keep burning in my mind and heart: "You fellows just don't know what you're talking about. You don't know the manner of spirit you are of; for the Son of

man came not to destroy men's lives, but to save them."
Don't you see, the zeal of the chosen people is of quite a
different dimension!

* * *

I try to understand the Lord, but it is not easy, for the
zealot reminds the theologian in me to pray for the fulfilment of prophecy. Unlike zealotry, prophecy has never
been my cup of tea, but I know the Scriptures telling
about Jesus being "revealed from heaven with his mighty
angels in blazing fire" (II Thessalonians 1:7), about the
heavens passing away "with a great rushing sound," the
elements melting in flames, and the earth and the works
that are upon it burning up (II Peter 3:10). Why not pray
for the fulfilment of a prophecy that appears to be tailor-
made for the nuclear era, and for the American dream?

Why not? I have never yet said Amen because it is too
easy to confuse the two functions of prophecy. Seen one
way, prophecy describes what will happen to man if he
does not follow the will of the Lord. Seen another way,
prophecy prescribes what is the will of the Lord and what
should happen. Heresy arises from the confusion of the
two functions.

Just because prophecy indicates that there will always
be sickness and death does not mean I should vote against
medicare, banish all the doctors, and close the hospitals.
Just because prophecy says there will be wars to the end
does not imply that I must hurry to press the nearest
button.

Quite the contrary! I must not forget the other prophecies—those which tell of man's sickness being healed, of
tears being wiped away, and of death coming no more!
Not only are there prophecies of fire raining down from
heaven, but also of heaven itself coming down, God dwell-
ing with men, and men beating their swords into plow-
shares (Revelation 21:1-4; Isaiah 2:1-4).

* * *

So I couldn't say Amen just for prophecy's sake. Still,
the educator and preacher in me are not satisfied, because
they have learned enough from psychotherapy to be fasci-
nated by the shock treatment.

The shock treatment may be a last resort, but when all other therapy has failed, why not use shock treatment? We know its effectiveness: the Germans and Japanese never did as much straight thinking as they did when we bombed the hell out of them. Only after fire rained down from heaven were they ready to forsake their national idolatries and shake their popular illusions.

Sometimes people are stirred up only when they are knocked off balance, when their props are pushed from underneath them, and they experience the shock of a lifetime. Some of our educational institutions, professors, and students need, more than anything else, such a shock treatment. So, too, our congregations. I have sometimes wondered whether a nuclear exchange would not be worth more than a million sermons. How else can people really be confronted by the madness of their present pursuits and the emptiness of their materialistic lives?

But I have not yet said Amen, because there is such a thing as shocking and shaking people to death. There can be one shock treatment too many. Besides, perhaps it is mostly the educator and preacher in me that needs shaking. I have not yet been instant in season and out of season. I have never preached in overalls like Ralph Abernathy, or in camel's hair like John the Baptist. I have never ridden on an ass into Jerusalem at the head of a massive demonstration, while Pilate and the high priest were looking on. And hellfire and brimstone have not been part of my vocabulary for a long time.

* * *

The reformer within me has also prayed for nuclear war, thinking that it could bring about the desired domestic and international order.

As Heinrich von Treitschki said, "God will see to it that war always recurs as a drastic medicine for the human race."[4] That sounds like a military officer in Saigon who told me that a new Vietnamese society would arise from the ruins of the war. After all, he said, sometimes it takes the complete destruction of a tradition and a social fabric to allow for the emergence of something new. Just compare Germany and England. The present fortunes of Germany lie in the past destruction of her cities, now rebuilt and entirely new. England is old and her cities are old because they were saved.

The officer did not mention Russian, Chinese, Canadian, and American cities, but his logic should perhaps be followed through, especially with respect to American cities. Consider: the ghettoes would be gone. The rats would be gone. The national guard would be gone. The people would be. . . .

Yes, the people would be gone too. That is why I have not said Amen to the military man in Saigon and to the reformer in me. Instead, I told him—and myself—that if all of us would get out of our military uniforms and put on overalls and lay down our weapons and pick up shovels, we could build a new Vietnam. And if even a part of the Pentagon budget were diverted to urban renewal, we would perhaps have new cities as well.

But what about the international order? Can the United Nations mature and graduate and federate the nations of this world so as to achieve the enforcement of international law and order? After all, it took the Napoleonic Wars to produce the 1815 Congress of Vienna; World War I to give birth to the League of Nations; World War II to bring forth the United Nations. Will it not take another conflagration to burn up forever the doctrine of the divine right of states in the same way that the doctrine of the divine right of kings was only destroyed by revolution and war? Perhaps it is true that the King of kings and Lord of lords can be seated on his throne only after all the empires—including the new Romans—have been crushed into the dust!

But I have not yet said Amen. Before I can finish my prayer, all of history, Christianity, and democracy enfolds before me, and I am confronted with questions not easily answered. Have history and wars not taught us enough? Does a universal Christian religion not provide motive power enough? Has democracy not commended itself enough to demand extension beyond a federation of states to a federation of nations and a republic of the world?

*   *   *

But then the militarist and pacifist within me remind me that first there must be order, and so it is best to fight the wars we must fight efficiently, end them conclusively, so that we can have peace, law, and order eternally.

Every man of war claims to be a man of peace; and every man of peace—if he feels strongly enough—often develops the motive power of war. They can sometimes be heard speaking together with Shakespeare:

> In God's name, cheerly on, courageous friends,
> To reap the harvest of perpetual peace
> By this one bloody trial of sharp war. [5]

Fight efficiently and get it over with. Why use a rusty knife when you have available a clean bomb? Why not, asks the militarist-pacifist within me, use that which allows men to die the quickest, cleanest, and completest way possible? Indeed, when one considers the options presented by the entire emerging weapons arsenal of nerve gases, blood gases, blister gases, choking gases, psychic poisons, infectious dust clouds, nuclear warfare may indeed be a coveted blessing.

But I cannot say Amen, because there is no "clean bomb." And it is not conventional, except in the dark recesses of the mind of those Pentagon generals for whom the difference between one man and a million is only half a dozen zeros. Nuclear war is not only quantitatively different; it is also qualitatively different. Moreover, the generals cannot tell me how they would solve the problems of Saigon by wiping out Hanoi, win Asia by destroying Indochina, or contain the wind of China by creating a power vacuum right near the storm center. I cannot say Amen because I fail to see how you can pave Vietnam and call it the American dream; how you can devise a "final solution" like the Germans and project a victory; how you can create a desert like the Romans and call it peace.

*   *   *

My God, have they ever got this thing all wrong. Yet they keep on saying it over and over again, these nuclear militarists, smooth and sorrowful as they are, pious and peaceful in their speech, yet with purposes more savage

21

than Genghis Khan. Their propaganda has found its way into every political campaign. One candidate would use conventional nuclear bombs. Another would delay ratification of the proliferation treaty. Another is unsure whether he would stop bombing or not.

Should we be surprised then that the propaganda is finding its way also into the prayers of the chaplains of the national religion? Some day, perhaps soon, these prayers will end with a unanimous Amen—unless you and I offer a religious and political alternative, take our pacifism into the streets, get busy about domestic and international reform, refine our theology, redirect our zeal, and wake up behind the pulpit and the lectern.

If we do not do this and much more, we will be praying, in effect, for a nuclear war. And sooner or later our prayers will be answered.

NOTES TO ESSAY I

1. "The Churches and the War in 1916," *The Canadian Annual Review*, 1917, p. 437.
2. *Thesaurus of Anecdotes* (Garden City: Doubleday, 1943), p. 415.
3. Mark Twain, "The War Prayer," *On the Damned Human Race* (New York: Hill and Wang, 1963), pp. 64-67.
4. Heinrich von Treitschki, *Politics*, I, 76.
5. Shakespeare, *Richard III*, Act V, scene 2, line 15.

II

On Being Afraid of Communism

"Perfect love casts out fear."
—I John 4:18

My sincere and completely serious taxi driver in Toronto
was most upset when a hurricane struck the State of Texas
some years ago with devastating effect. He was not as
troubled by the terror in the South as by a strong feeling
that the storms in Texas were responsible for the miserable
weather in Toronto. Since I had observed how political
winds blowing out of Texas—Lyndon Johnson was then
the US President—were affecting the national climate in
Canada, I let his weather theory stand, at least as an
analogy, recognizing that weather systems around the
world are interdependent.

His interpretation was interesting also as a contrast to
the American weather reports I had heard so often during
my student days in Kansas and Minnesota. I remembered
that the weathermen in those states would, with irritating
regularity, blame climatic conditions on the mass of air,
usually cold, blowing in from Canada, and beyond Canada,
no doubt, from Siberia.

The weathermen did not actually suggest that Communism was responsible for the frosty drafts, but my taxi
driver insisted that it was the cause of the unwanted winds.
He had read in a magazine that either the Chinese or
Russians or both were responsible for the many hurricanes

hitting the American shores. The winds originated over there somewhere—at least the Communists knew exactly how to unsettle the weather and stir up such storms! The name of the magazine he couldn't remember, but I did not doubt his word, knowing that hundreds of such publications have for years blamed Communism for everything seen as adverse—weather, religion, politics, integrated schools, chlorinated water, or medicare.

In the late forties, fifties, and early sixties we heard repeatedly about "the threat of Communism," and church publications sponsored essay contests on "What a teen-ager today can do about the threat of Communism." The threat has not seemed to be as prominent lately. Professional anti-Communists have had rough going, especially since President Richard Nixon's visits to Peking and Moscow. But it takes little to give new fuel to the crusaders of fear. It was Czechoslovakia in 1968 that led *Christian Century* to editorialize:

> We predict . . . a good year for Red baiting, that the perennial revival of the Red terror as the guiding spectre of American political life is upon us again.[1]

Not a few politicians have ridden high on the wave of hysteria and the people's paranoid fear of Communism. Their exploitation of fear brings a measure of short-term political success, but in the end, extreme anxiety and mistrust produce the very conditions they were meant to avert. This, no doubt, is why Franklin D. Roosevelt, in his first inaugural address in 1933, told his economically depressed countrymen: " . . . the only thing we have to fear is fear itself—nameless, unreasoning, unjustified terror which paralyzes needed efforts to convert retreat into advance."

The paralytic effect of fear was probably also the reason why John the Apostle told first-century Christians, constantly threatened by totalitarian enemies of all sorts, that the conquest of fear was not only desirable but necessary and possible:

> There is no fear in love, but perfect love casts out fear. For fear has to do with punishment, and he who fears is not perfected in love (I John 4:18).

From that saying we conclude that fear is outside of Christian perfection, and that anyone who would mature must get rid of fear. Thomas Carlyle said that "the first duty of man is that of subduing fear."[2] But how may we live above the hysteria of our time? How is it possible not to be afraid of Communism? Let me suggest some possibilities by paraphrasing the Apostle in seven different ways.

*   *   *

First of all, we might recognize in all humility that Communism is an historical judgment on Christianity. Penitent admission of this fact could cast out much of our fear.

Russell Mast has correctly pointed out that Communism has made progress in one country after another where it has come as a hope to masses of people victimized by injustice and oppression, when it has come as a substitute for religion to a people who have lost meaning in their lives, and for whom religion has become cold and formal and empty. He concludes, "If in Communism we see the result of what we have not been doing, the fruit of our neglect, then only a deeply felt attitude of penitence becomes us now."[3] In certain countries at least Communism is a judgment on what was a sterile religion lacking social concern and on Christianity's unholy alliances with established military, economic, and governmental authorities, which together have fought to preserve their privileges instead of cooperating to bring the good life to oppressed people.

A recognition of this and a confession of our fault could release us from the fear that comes when we do not face the truth and admit our guilt.

Perfect humility casts out fear.

*   *   *

Secondly, we might acknowledge some notable Communist achievements. Perfect honesty about Communism could cast out some of our fear.

Henrik Frederic Amiel, writing in his *Journal* for March 1869, more than a century ago, observed that men are governed "by the fear of truth." This observation applies as well to Western man's appraisal of Communism, about which he has not always been honest. If he could recognize and admit that Communism has some notable sociological achievements to its credit his fear could be substantially reduced.

There are many things, of course, that Communism has not achieved, and some of the achievements have come at a tremendous price. But there have been achievements. In Soviet Russia, equal opportunity and free education have become a reality for millions of formerly impoverished and unfree serfs. In China, no less than 700 million people are fed with only limited domestic resources and limited outside help. In Cuba, widespread illiteracy has actually been eliminated in a single decade. And in French Indochina the struggle for freedom and independence from foreigners, an independence which was later betrayed by other foreigners, was led by Communists.

I am certain that there are those who would like to debate even this short, and by no means exhaustive, list. But let those who would debate it strive above all to be honest.

Perfect honesty, no matter where it leads, casts out fear.

* * *

Thirdly, our fears could be reduced by a further look at Communist realities. A more perfect knowledge of these realities could cast out much of our remaining fear.

Most of what we think and feel about Communism we know second-hand from the endless oversimplifications and repetitions of the propaganda people, who speak of Communism as a monolith, a single unified force or power bloc that is threatening our culture. With them there is no differentiation between the Communisms of the various nation-states.

Yet, such differentiation is necessary if we would have perfect knowledge. As Arnold Toynbee advises:

> All over the world today the predominant ideology is neither communism nor free enterprise: it is nationalism. Today, the nationalism of the non-western peoples is pitted against the nationalism of the western peoples. The revolt of the native majority of mankind against the domination of the western minority—this, and not the defence of freedom against

communism by the leading western country, the United States, is the real major issue in the world today.[4]

Most Americans have not yet recognized this reality, and that is why they are afraid. The very revolutionary force that two hundred years ago made them a nation, that King George III could not suppress, is today stirring peoples all over the world. That force is to be feared only if, like George III, one is opposed to it, not if one is allied to it. But even if one is opposed to it, one should at least recognize that the force is also a modifier, if not a destroyer, of Communism.

The nationalisms of countries like Czechoslovakia will always give Europe more security from Soviet domination than the military forces of NATO. The nationalisms of countries like Vietnam will "contain China" better than any ring of Western military bases.

Better knowledge of these facts could free us from our fear.

* * *

We could, in the fourth place, be helped if we could see God at work in Communist countries in spite of, or because of, or alongside of, Communism. A perfect faith could cast out our fear.

Those who see Communism as a monolithic power often also credit it with the status, omnipotence, and immutability of God. Unwittingly, they give to Communism a strength it does not possess and a destiny it can never obtain.

They cannot conceive of the spirit of God producing a vital and transforming faith in a Communist country, nor can they imagine the processes of education demanding a liberalization of even the most dictatorial regimes. Yet, if they would open their eyes, they would see this very thing happening before them in their time. Where this is not evident to the physical eye it should be evident to the eyes of faith. Eyes of faith can see that the sun of Christian glory may yet rise in the East. By faith they see that the strong tradition of religion in Russia, the trial by fire of that religion in the twentieth century, the faithfulness of many courageous witnesses, and the social emphases of the political ideology may be used by the Spirit to bring about a vibrant and relevant Christianity that will be difficult to duplicate in the decadent and materialistic West.

Gandhi once said, "Where there is fear, there is no religion!" We might add that where there is religious faith there need be no fear.

Perfect faith casts out all fear.

* * *

In the fifth place, let us return to the exact words of our text. A reduction of our prejudice, hate, and selfishness could make us less fearful. Perfect love casts out fear.

In our reference to love we actually face a paradox, because love, depending on the object of our love, can do both, increase our fears and reduce them.

Where love of self is high, fear escalates, because the forces we have identified as Communism threaten the usual objects of our self-love: property, power, privileged position as a racial minority, social status. If we could reduce this love of property, power, and privilege, our fears would immediately diminish. In fact, if we could (as Jesus would have us) will a sacrificial share of our resources to the rest of humanity and see ourselves as servants, our fears might disappear completely. If we could then proceed a step further and love our enemies and pray for those who would abuse us, we would be free from fear for certain. Then even the cross would not frighten us.

Perfect love casts out all fear.

* * *

Closely related to faith and love is hope, the quality of life that extends beyond the here and now of physical existence. Hope has a way of chasing away any remaining fears.

Hope is a match for our fears even when Communism takes the terrible form of Stalinism and the Communist way of life is full of one-way streets to death in a Siberian labor camp.

I can imagine the disciples of Jesus accepting only reluctantly their Master's teachings on the incompatibility of fear and faith, as again and again he would pose new possibilities, including Stalinism. The Master would not, could not, change his line. "Do not fear those who kill the body, but cannot kill the soul. Fear him rather who is able to destroy both soul and body in hell . . ." (Matthew 10:28).

It almost seems that today this kind of fearlessness has to be taught to the Christian world by the guerillas whose cause is so real and whose hope is so firm that neither bombs from inaudible and invisible B-52s nor cannisters of napalm released just above the tree tops can discourage them in their struggle. It is easier for them to have their bodies killed than to have their souls prostituted by the enemies of their humanity.

When people's lives are without hope and full of fear they build up a weapons arsenal that could wipe out the rest of the human race just to save their own bodies. And yet their fear remains. Could it be that they who would save our bodies are the real enemies of our souls? Could it be that their fear remains because their insecurity is within, because they have no hope?

More hope means less fear; indeed, a perfect hope could rid us of all our fear.

*   *   *

Humility, honesty, and knowledge, faith, love, and hope are the ingredients of courage. And where there is courage, fear has been overcome.

Fear and courage are two different responses to life situations. The Warsaw Pact invasion of Czechoslovakia in 1968 provides a good recent example.

The response of fear—whether in Germany or Canada or the USA—was that NATO had to be strengthened. Military maneuvers began once again. Fear, which has a logic all its own, also demanded an immediate start on the $5 billion anti-missile system, even though its original justification was to meet the Chinese threat. But Czechoslovakian courage kept its 175,000 guns in holster and decided to react in the only way that a meaningful long-term victory could be assured—with endurance and long-suffering and courage.

"Have no fear of them," we hear the Master advising:

> I send you out like sheep among wolves. . . . Be on your guard, for men will hand you over to their courts, they will flog you in the synagogues, and you will be brought before governors

and kings, for my sake. . . . So do not be afraid of them. . . . What I say to you in the dark you must repeat in broad daylight; what you hear whispered you must shout from the house-tops (Matthew 10:16-18, 26-27).

In effect he was saying that there will be oppressions and invasions. He does not promise to stop them, but he does offer the gift of courage. Perfect courage makes no allowance for fear.

*   *   *

The worst is yet to come. Those who have no humility, no honesty, no knowledge, no faith, no love, and no hope, but only fear to offer the American people, are moving to take control. As the horizons darken and the skies blacken—and blacken they surely will before they brighten— remember the words of Czech Theologian Jan Milic Lochman: "Tanks are potent but they are not omnipotent."[5] Or the words of Elmer Davis: "The first commandment is: don't let them scare you!"[6]

And the words of the Apostle John: "Perfect love casts out fear."

NOTES TO ESSAY II

1. "Universal Moral Myopia," *The Christian Century*, September 4, 1968, p. 1095.

2. Thomas Carlyle, "Heroes and Hero-worship," in George Seldes, *The Great Quotations* (New York: Simon & Schuster, 1967), p. 355.

3. Russell Mast, *Christianity and Communism* (Newton, Kansas: Faith and Life, 1962), p. 25.

4. Arnold Toynbee, "Communism Not Real Issue—It's Revolt Against Domination." Mimeographed article originally appearing in *The London Observer.*

5. Quoted in *The New York Times*, September 22, 1968.

6. Elmer Davis, *But We Were Born Free.*

III

Evangelism and Peace

"How blest are the peacemakers;
God shall call them his sons."
—Matthew 5:9

Do evangelism and peace belong together in the Christian
program and proclamation? I believe the answer is yes.
Many Christian teachings and many biblical texts assume
an obvious and natural relationship between the Christian
peace witness and Christian evangelism. Consider, for instance, Jesus' words from the Sermon on the Mount cited
at the head of this essay.

Not all Christian people would agree. There are some
who are fond of quoting texts, especially from the Old
Testament, that seem to justify war and make patriotism,
even a militaristic patriotism, an obligation of Christian
believers.

Thus it happens in our time that peace and evangelism
appear in juxtaposition more often than not and that the
distance between the two is often unbridgeable. This is not
a new phenomenon, as we know from Roland Bainton's
historical survey of *Christian Attitudes Toward War and
Peace.* The modern evangelist who waves the flag while he
preaches the cross, who equates the wars of his nation with
the Christian attack on evil, who calls his mass audience to
decide at one and the same time for both God and country, as though they were synonymous, has numerous prec-

31

edents in history. Since Constantine the Great evangelism has often been the handmaiden of state religion.

That it is according to an historical pattern, however, does not make it right. The time has come, I believe, for Christian believers to take a second look at the traditional behavior. Tradition is not always truth, and what society considers normal is in God's sight not always moral. Let us examine once more the foundations of our faith and the relationships between peace and evangelism. We shall do it in this essay from three vantage points—theology, sociology, and psychology—that is, from the points of view of God, the world, and man.

* * *

First of all, we can observe that peace and evangelism come together, inseparably linked, when we consider the person of Christ.

If evangelism has to do with the calling of people to become followers of Christ—and it does—we must concern ourselves not only with the method of that call but also, and mostly, with the content of that call. The content is the evangel, the good news that Christ is redeemer and leader of men. With Paul, the church through the ages has summarized its proclamation ministry in these succinct words: *"We proclaim Christ . . . "* (I Corinthians 1 :23).

But there are many christs who have come into this world. The invitation wholeheartedly to accept Jesus Christ assumes that a proper identification has been made of the Christ to be accepted. That Christ can be, and is, variously interpreted should be clear to us from history, and from contemporary culture, in which Jesus has become the easy theme of mass circulation magazines.

The popularity of Jesus in the folk and rock music of our time is sufficient reminder that not all who name Christ mean Christ, though more do than we are probably prepared to recognize, with our meanings tied as they are to favorite cultural and linguistic forms. In any event, the most serious misrepresentations of Christ are not to be found in the counter culture or rock hymnody. Much greater distortions of Christ flourish in the serious and sacred history of establishment culture, which at various times has refashioned Christ as the champion of capitalism, the advocate of racism, the missionary of imperialism, and the chaplain of militarism. Indeed, so much has the name of Christ been abused that it may become necessary for us to use his name less so that we may preach him more.

Much greater than the problem of language, however, has been the theological distortion that identifies the cruci-fied Christ as the way *to* life and not the way *of* life, and forgets that the two emphases are inseparable parts of each other and that the "doctrine of the cross . . . is the power of God" for the whole of life (I Corinthians 1:18-24).

In Jesus' own theology, the accepted cross was not first of all an automatic pass to the golden highways of heaven but a style of life on the grimy byways of earth. His evangelistic call, found in all three Synoptic Gospels, made this clear. Take up your cross and follow me (see Matthew 16:24; Mark 8:34; Luke 9:23).

But again, it is not just any cross, not the cross of Constantine, which turned Christ into a military con-queror, but the cross of Isaiah, who identified Christ as "the suffering servant," and of the New Testament writers who proclaimed him as "the Lamb of God . . . who takes away the sins of the world" (John 1:29). The cross is a cross, not a gun. Christ is a servant, not a slave-driver. The lamb is a lamb, not a wolf. His spirit is that of a dove, not a hawk—and not an eagle!

Nonresistance is integral to the character of Christ and can, therefore, be considered normative for his followers. In his Sermon on the Mount Jesus characterized the saved sons of God as peacemakers, merciful people who love their enemies and pray for their persecutors, turning the other cheek, going the second mile, surrendering the sec-ond coat, always seeking on earth the will of God as it is already applied in heaven.

The biblical visionaries also saw Christ as the suffering Savior by whom and through whom all wars could, should, and would come to an end. Isaiah proclaimed him as a "Prince of Peace" whose expanding, never-ending govern-ment would capture all hearts and encompass the whole world (9:6). John represented him as the Lamb, whose policies of peace the nations learned to accept and by whose light they walked (Revelation 21:22-24). Paul saw

33

Christ as the reconciler of all things, "making peace through the shedding of his blood upon the cross" (Colossians 1:20).

*   *   *

Second, we note that peace and evangelism are inseparably linked when we view the condition of the society in which we evangelize.

Evangelism has to do with salvation. This is variously described in the sacred writings. For Ezekiel it meant a new heart and a new spirit for man, a heart of flesh in exchange for the one of stone (36:26). John preferred to speak about the new birth (John 1:13; 3:3) and Paul about the new creature (II Corinthians 5:17). All emphasized an internal reorientation of the mind and heart, a wholehearted surrender of life toward the service of mankind and the glory of God. Salvation replaced alienation with reconciliation, hate with love, wickedness with righteousness. In the renewal experience, the penitent had their sins forgiven and their souls set on imitating Christ.

Both sin and virtue, however, are very abstract terms, necessarily so because they refer to intangible qualities and spiritual essence. Yet they have their visible manifestations and concrete expressions, though varying from time to time and place to place. This is why prophets and evangelists have found it necessary and desirable to speak to the people about sin and virtue in terms of their human, social, and earthly manifestations.

Some of the biblical lists of sins are quite familiar. We know the very down-to-earth treatment in the Ten Commandments, where unclean language, abuse of holy days, disrespectfulness toward parents, killing, adultery, stealing, lying, and false witnessing are condemned (Exodus 20:1-17). The prophets were particularly concerned with economic exploitation and social injustice—the devouring of widows' houses, the lack of concern for orphans, the abuse of religious festivals, the absence of truth, mercy, and knowledge in the land, the swearing, lying, killing, stealing, adultery, and the spilling of blood (Isaiah 1; Hosea 4:1, 2). Paul's list has been classic for the church: "fornication, impurity, and indecency; idolatry and sorcery; quarrels, a contentious temper, envy, fits of rage, selfish ambitions, dissensions, party intrigues, and jealousies; drinking bouts, orgies, and the like" (Galatians 5:19-21).

Other post-apostolic Christian leaders translated sin and virtue into the problems and needs of their day. The Dutch Reformer Menno Simons, for instance, was no generalizer. Among lords and princes he found vanity, arrogance, pomp and pride, banqueting, eating and drinking to excess, adultery, fornication, and blind idolatry. He named them tyrannical, haughty like Nebuchadnezzar, drunk like Belshazzar, and bloodthirsty like Nero.

Our day is really no different. Every evangelist must have his list of sins. And the character of the salvation and renewal he brings to a community depends not only on how he illuminates the character of Christ but also on how he defines sin and virtue. All of us can identify communities where the coming of the evangelist meant the emptying of movie houses, the burning of books, the plowing of tobacco fields, the melting down of jewelry, and the closing of saloons.

Let no one underestimate the social influence of evangelists. They have changed the language, the liturgy, and the hymnody of entire communities; they have helped or hindered ecumenicity on a grand scale; they have upset or strengthened economies, destroyed and built institutions, ruined and boosted personalities. The question confronting us when we consider evangelists and evangelism, therefore, is not whether they have an effect but rather what kind of effect, not whether they have lists of sins but whether those lists are adequate.

In our time the agenda of Christian evangelism has been strangely devoid of reference to one of the greatest and most frequent manifestations of sin in the twentieth century—war. This is the century of world wars, yet surprisingly enough evangelism, with few exceptions, finds no relevance for its task in that condition. Where evangelists are not (at their worst) supporting the national mood and leading the flag-waving, they are (at their best) silent.

In no other area is this so well illustrated as with respect to war, especially the US war in Indochina. Few wars have brought so much deception, bloodletting, exploitation, corruption, and waste, so much murder, drug addiction, and prostitution, so much wholesale destruction of man, woman, and child, of plant and animal life, over such a long period of time as this war. Never has a people who have had the benefit of so much Christianity, so much university education, so much "free" press, and so much revolutionary political doctrine—committed such a barbarism.

The evangelists who closed the saloons, shut the theaters down, and plowed the tobacco fields under could have stopped this war. As it was, not a few of them provided the religious energy to keep it going. And all because they failed to see the connection between the moral salvation task of evangelism and the immoral condition of society and its members.

* * *

Finally, we observe a natural and necessary relationship between peace and evangelism as we consider the nature of true communication.

Quite understandably, the church has been impatient to get on with the monumental task of preaching the gospel in the whole world. Its search for shortcuts to the conversion of all of humanity has often led to the use of pressure and force, as we know from church history. Physical force led to the "conversion" of the heathen at the point of a sword, to mass baptisms through enforced river marches, and to doctrinal submission at the risk of heresy trials and persecutions. The Crusades remain a classic example of the employment of force to advance the kingdom.

The time came when such tactics were considered inappropriate to conversion, but frequently they were replaced by a social and economic organization of society that left little room for escape. Humanity became a captive child of the church, as in Catholic Europe before the Reformation and as in Calvinist and Lutheran Europe after the Reformation. In these and other situations there was hardly a way the individual could fail to conform and still survive.

In our modern pluralistic society we have finally conceded the Anabaptist principle that free men must make

36

voluntary choices. But again an impatient church has suc-
cumbed to grave temptation. More often than not it has
followed the example of the mass persuaders in politics,
business, and entertainment to see how the world might be
converted in one generation.

All that is needed, we are led to assume, is organizational genius, technological finesse, and psychological
force. We have become so impressed with the thunder-
storms of Madison Avenue evangelism that we forget its
erosive effects on the "land," its superficial wetting of the
surface, its quick runoff into muddy rivers, and its harden-
ing of the soil. We barely realize how badly our society
needs the steady, thorough soaking of the gentle, hardly
noticeable rain, the silence of the warming sunshine, and
the cooling flow of a clean, fresh breeze. So impressed
have we become with technology, force, and spectacle that
we have neglected, if not largely destroyed, the solid
education and nurture programs in home, church, and
school. We have, in effect, proceeded to weed our gardens
with bulldozers and to water our flower plots with the
high pressure hoses of fire trucks.

Free men, women, and children making free choices
must not thus be pressurized, brain-washed, psychologically forced. The gentle rain, the warming sun, the refreshing breeze, and the open sky still remain the best physical
analogies of how God works in the world of the spirit. In
that world doves descend quietly, flames appear noiselessly, and winds blow invisibly, bringing men to newness
of life in ways so varied that salvation experience cannot
easily be categorized, certainly not computerized.

This brings us back to content as related to Christ and
the condition of the world. Our crusades are especially
disastrous when it comes to winning the questioning young
of our own society and the awakening masses of the wider
world. We knew once that we could not go to India as
missionaries without first responding to famine. And we
know now that we cannot preach the gospel anywhere in
the world if our preaching is not first of all through
agriculture where people are hungry, medicine where there
is disease, education where there is illiteracy, brotherliness
where there is segregation. Yet, in a century of world wars
and in a global village, where we offer billions of dollars

worth of military hardware for the bread of human subsistence, we hope to get a hearing without addressing ourselves to this wicked condition.

We should not be surprised if the Vietnamese finally decide against Christianity as the Chinese and the Russians already have done and as the Indians are in the process of doing. There will be those who blame the Communists for closing the doors, but the closing will have been largely our doing. If the crucified Christ comes through to them as a crucifier, exploiting and enslaving them rather than saving them in their condition, how will they listen and how can they accept?

And the Lord will say to us as he has always said to religion that lacked relevant substance: " . . . Assemblies, sacred seasons and ceremonies, I cannot endure. I cannot tolerate . . . your festivals. . . . Though you offer countless prayers, I will not listen. There is blood on your hands . . . " (Isaiah 1:13-15).

*   *   *

Peace and evangelism come together in a true communication of the self-giving Christ to a warring world—at least in theory. In practice there are problems, obviously, because in the culture of our time both have become quite detached from their Christian moorings and from each other.

It should, however, be possible to bring them together again. A fuller theology of Christ demands it. A truer sociology of this world requires it. The deeper psychology of man desires it. The church can facilitate it by giving to evangelism not more strategy, but more substance, the substance of the gospel of peace, through sound preaching, strong teaching, and never-ending labors of love.

IV

Evangelism and Visions of a New World

> *"Then I saw a new heaven and a new earth. . . .*
> *And I saw the holy city, new Jerusalem, coming*
> *down out of heaven from God. . . ."*
>
> —Revelation 21:1-2

In theory at least, evangelism and revolution have much in common. Both imply dissatisfaction with the *status quo;* both have visions of a new state of being; both seek to make "all things new," to use the biblical phrase (Revelation 21:5). And, as a consequence, both evangelists and revolutionaries usually assume that they are bearers of good news for men.

What is true in theory, however, is not always true in practice, because neither evangelism nor revolution ever appears in pure form. Revolution is often little more than a *coup d'etat*, the overthrow of one power structure by another, both of which pursue essentially the same selfish ends and employ the same violent and nonrevolutionary means. Evangelism presents a similar problem. Its language has undergone changes in meaning, and its institutions have undergone changes in role. Once evangelism stressed the good news, the substance of change; now it often stresses the strategy. Once it was an instrument of dynamic renewal in society; now it quite often serves the function of preserving the *status quo.*

Once evangelists were prophets, preaching justice to

kings whose hands were dripping with blood. Now many of them lend dignity and sanctity to the "hail Caesar" days. As baptism or confirmation has in certain societies become a social rite, so evangelism has become the essential liturgy of civil religion. For all of these reasons it will not be easy to relate evangelism and visions of a new world order, but we must make the effort.

*   *   *

The problem of evangelism today is not that it has no vision, but that its vision is incomplete, or somehow not properly related to the world, or both. Evangelism has its visions of a saved soul and an eternal heaven, both of them rather revolutionary notions, but between the two is a great gulf. When confronted by the challenge of discovering the gospel's relevance to the social order, evangelicals usually excuse themselves from responsibility by invoking a doctrine called "the separation of church and state" without clearly knowing or indicating what that means. Sometimes it appears to be a separation of time from eternity, or earth from heaven; at other times of the body from the soul, the individual from society, and God from humanity. By convincing ourselves that the desired separation is possible, we as evangelicals can accept for ourselves the convenient implications of the gospel and reject or opt out of whatever comes in conflict with our positions of comfort and respectability.

The separation of church and state, we take for granted, was a unique revelation of the Protestant Reformation, and it may well have been, but it surely became distorted in the evangelical tradition. Whereas separation in the beginning meant that the church maintained a prophetic and critical stance toward the state, the same slogan was later used to mean exactly the opposite. Today evangelists and politicians become easy bedfellows and readily use each other's platforms to reinforce each other's purposes. When it comes to applying the sharp edge of the gospel, however, both become champions of separation.

A great relevance gulf has developed between God and the world, between the gospel and a vision, between the church and society. Somewhere in the past this began by the formal separation of church and state. It continued as we also separated church and business, church and labor, and church and leisure. We began by explicitly preaching the separation of church and state and ended by implicitly teaching the separation of Sunday and Monday, of heaven and earth, of eternity and time, of faith and life, of God and humanity, of church and society. The end result of this separation was disclosed by the Canadian Institute of Public Opinion, which reported that most Canadian Christians believe the church has nothing to say about nuclear weapons and tests.

There are distinctions to be made between these various entities, to be sure. Church and state are not the same. But that does not make the one unrelated to the other. The separation of church and state cannot mean that Jesus Christ is not Lord of both church and state, or that the church has nothing to say by way of declaring the Lordship of Christ in and over this world, because Christ becomes the Savior of the world only when he becomes its Lord.

We believe today that God has a will, a plan, a desired destiny for all of society. We confess this faith every time we pray "Thy will be done, on earth as it is in heaven." Heaven here is the model of the perfect society, the realm where God's will is already being done. This will God wants done in this world, on earth. The discovery of that will is revelation. Its sighting is a vision. Its proclamation is prophecy and evangelism. Without it there is no evangel, even though we may still be "evangelizing."

* * *

Although evangelicals lost their concern in the great separation, the vision itself was not lost. God did not leave himself without witnesses. His spirit kept breathing on the face of the earth. He caused the winds of change to keep blowing from the world's four corners. And when his chosen ones failed him, he raised up children and visionaries among the stones of the desert.

To the extent that the vision was missing among the evangelicals, it had to come from elsewhere. Early in the twentieth century it came from the advocates of so-called "progressive Christianity." Evangelicals assigned these visionaries negative labels; they spoke disparagingly of the "social gospel" and "liberalism," thereby doing injustice to both the vision and the visionaries.

The father of the social gospel, Walter Rauschenbusch, was completely written off by evangelicals who forgot that he not only proclaimed a social gospel but also a personal gospel, and for him both were part of each other. His volume of *Evangeliumslieder* (gospel songs) was as fundamental to his viewpoint as were his other works, notably *Christianizing the Social Order.* Similarly, they turned a deaf ear to Harry Emerson Fosdick, even though he too saw salvation starting on the inside of man and moving out into the environment. To use his own words:

> The characteristic approach of the Christian gospel to the human problem is from within out; the characteristic approach of much of the modern social movement is from without in. . . . Upon this master fact that men can be inwardly transformed, Christ laid his hand and put it at the very center of the gospel. . . . It is the more strange that this central element in the Christian gospel should be neglected in the interest of social reformation because it is so indispensable to social reformation.[1]

God also had his witnesses outside of the church. As he used the humanists to prepare Europe for the Reformation, he has often used "way out" people to prepare the way for the coming of his kingdom.

In our time, is it not true that God has used the Communists to remind Christianity of its economic vision? Or the scientists to insist that he really wants to come down out of the heavens to dwell among people? Or the peace movement to remind us of Isaiah's vision of the Prince of Peace whose government has no end? Or civil rights leaders (violent or nonviolent) to reveal to us the equality of all men? Or the world federalists to make the point that there is a higher sovereignty than that of the nation-state? Or resurgent Eastern religions to emphasize humility, humanity, and spirituality in the face of Western religions that idolize efficiency and technology? Or even atheists to remind us that we often worship gods of our own image?

To consider that revelation comes from such sources is

for most of us quite a heretical thought, but God cannot be without witnesses. It is high time for us to examine the contents of a witness before we pass judgment on the basis of labels. We do not make people, events, or ideas Christian by giving them the name, nor can we make them un-Christian by using non-Christian name tags. Modern-day visionaries may themselves be in need of receiving all the good news, but they will not receive what is missing if our communication denies them that which they already have of Christ and his kingdom. True evangelism in these situations begins more with open ears than with open mouths. The evangelistic package of good news may not be limited to a detached-from-the-world, peace-in-the-heart message of pie-in-the-sky. We must either bridge the gulf with a fuller vision or get out of the way.

The so-called nonevangelical or even non-Christian visionaries, it is true, do not always recognize the ultimate source of their vision. And sometimes their strengths in some areas are more than offset by weaknesses in other areas. But it is also true that many of them, like Marx and Gandhi, reject Christianity though they have learned much from Christ, because Christianity as they know it rejects the Christian vision they embrace.

The race issue in North America is perhaps the best illustration of how our vision of the equality of man received its contemporary thrust not from evangelical preaching but rather from secular prophets, mostly the US Supreme Court. Even today, racial integration in evangelical circles is little more than tokenism. Institutional racism is rarely, if ever, attacked. There are exceptions to the rule, of course. The first recorded protest in the American colonies "that the slave trade flaunted Christian principles" was made by the Germantown Mennonites and Quakers.[2] Unfortunately, the Mennonites, like most other evangelical groups, did not remain true to the original vision, and the more they became wedded to the system the more they appealed to "the separation of church and state" to escape their responsibility and to cover up the immorality of racism. Thus, the church, according to Dean Liston Pope, became "the most segregated major institution in American society."

It has lagged behind the Supreme Court as the conscience of the nation on questions of race, and it has fallen far behind trade unions, factories, schools, department stores, athletic gatherings and most other major areas of human association. . . .[3]

There are two sides to the story, of course. The one side is that Christianity and its much maligned social gospel was the leaven that leavened the lump, the redemptive force that prepared the climate for the Supreme Court decision. The other is that a retarded Christian vision held up racial redemption as long as it could and as long as it did. And we must underline *retarded*, because as late as 1864 one large US denomination insisted that "it is the peculiar mission of the Southern church to conserve the institution of slavery."[4] Ninety years later, following on the heels of the Supreme Court, that denomination had the courage to reverse itself, as it affirmed that "enforced segregation of the races is discrimination which is out of harmony with Christian theology and ethics. . . ."[5]

Why did the evangelical denominations and spokesmen trail rather than inspire the secular prophets? And why do they continue to do so today on race and other issues, unwilling to accept the biblical vision on the one hand, and condemning the secular visions which have their origin in God on the other? I am convinced that one of these decades we evangelicals will oppose war and militarism, but unfortunately we will do so not as leaders but as confused followers. Usually we wait until a vision has become safe and respectable.

The situation would be less sad if we would admit that the problem lies with our lack of conviction and courage. But instead of admitting our own weaknesses, we invoke the great separation and read the great vision out of the Bible.

* * *

The absence of lofty visions of a new world order in evangelical Christianity is not due to an absence of such visions in the inspired writings of the Old and the New Testaments. On the contrary, very few of man's great dreams for society are excluded from the biblical literature, though the extent of their treatment varies a great deal. All the cities and utopias about which man has dreamed have their prototypes in the Scriptures.

To be sure, nowhere in the biblical literature do we find a complete and comprehensive review of God's new order. Visions rarely appear in the form of detailed blueprints or systematic theologies. None of the inspired writers saw the whole thing, at least not all of the time. The most humble of them admitted that at best they saw "puzzling reflections" (I Corinthians 13:12) and that they hoped some day to see things face to face. Yet the glimpses they did catch of the city of God among men are most significant, because for us, as they were for them, they are an essential part of the good news.

One of the most beautifully expressed visions is Isaiah's. He saw the coming both of a Prince of Peace, whose government would have no end, and of a warless world. This vision has been engraved on the walls of the UN building in New York. More importantly, it is a vision that has moved many men and women to become partners with God in removing from this planet one of its foremost evils, war. Isaiah indicates that this will come about if and when the tribalisms and nationalisms of this world recognize a sovereignty greater than their own.

Some people have seen in this imagery a strengthened United Nations or a world federation of nations, an interpretation evangelicals have tended to resist as unrepresentative of the Lord of lords and King of kings. Their critique has its validity, but it loses its credibility when these same evangelicals turn around and recruit that King of kings as the Commander-in-Chief of nationalistic forces, even for fighting their most dirty wars. The UN and world federalism are obviously not the highest visions, but they are much higher than can be found among evangelical nationalists today.

Confronted by Isaiah's vision, we have sought to escape its implications. We have spiritualized it, millennialized it, or removed it from our lives by some other separation. There will always be wars, we said, as we quoted Jesus, and as we turned his description of how man behaves into a prescription of how he ought to behave. Curiously enough, we do not apply that approach to other similar scourges of man. We know that like war we will also have sickness and death to the end, but we close none of our hospitals, nor do we in any way depreciate medical science. On the contrary, we accord the medical profession the highest status and willingly allot to practitioners the highest fees. Meanwhile, those who become professional workers for peace often lose their salaries, receive the worst social labels, and not infrequently are put in jail. We know we can never be missionaries to Asia and Africa without a vision for an end to sickness and hunger, but somehow we try to evangelize the world without a vision for ending war or economic disparity.

Another prominent biblical vision overlooked by evangelicals has to do with economics. We have given much energy and theology to defending one economic system in preference to another, little realizing that our laws on property, related as they are to violent conquest and purely commercial considerations, fall far short of the economic vision of the biblical revelation. The most fundamental expression of that vision was formulated by David:

> The earth is the Lord's
> and all that is in it,
> the world and those who dwell therein ... (Psalm 24:1).

David did not know the whole earth and its wealth, as we know it today, and yet he saw that all the resources belonged to God, which means to all the people of this earth of all time. This vision comes to the fore again and again in the Bible. We see the first man acknowledging his original stewardship, Moses drawing up his laws to protect both land and people, prophets denouncing the devouring of widows' houses, Jesus telling the rich to distribute to the poor, the church establishing a community of economic justice, and John predicting a time when none will hunger nor thirst.

This vision has not followed us or been part of our evangelism. Instead, we are quite blind to God's plan and the world's reality. We cry "Communist" whenever the vision or reality is presented to us. Americans pride themselves in being "the most generous nation in history"[6] and forget completely that the rich, who exploit both resources and people, are usually generous.

At the same time we overlook the fact that our generosity becomes a damning deficit when we also add up the ill-begotten gains from selfish trade practices, unfair investment policies, and deceptive aid programs. No nation has ever burned up so disproportionate a share of the world's present and future resources for the benefit of such a small group of people as has America.

The warless world and the just economy are two samples of God's good news related to the new world order. There are others in the biblical revelation, visions of a new humanity (Ephesians 4:13f.), the perfection of justice (Acts 17:31), the liberation of creation (Romans 8:20-21), the healing of the nations (Revelation 21:24—22:2), the renewal of urban society (Revelation 21:10-11), unsegregated and classless community (Revelation 7:9; 21:1), the completion of knowledge (I Corinthians 13:12), the perfection of communication (Revelation 7:9-12).

In our zeal to expand our vision, we must be careful not to swallow too easily the assumptions of our society, especially of those technocratic visionaries who see salvation in cybernetics and who look to the computer for the perfection of knowledge and communication. Technology can be our limited servant, but today it is in danger of becoming our master, and an insidious master at that. The computer could become for us the ultimate instrument of deception if we program it with the gross distortions characteristic of current propaganda.

Perhaps the most misunderstood biblical vision is that called the kingdom, the concept Jesus chose to describe the totality of the new man, the new order, and the new age.[7] His kingdom represented a reality different from, and greater than, the Roman imperial kingdom, the Jewish national kingdom, or the Pharisees' religious kingdom. All of them understood that their old orders were threatened by the coming of Christ's kingdom, and that is why they accused the Galilean visionary of getting involved in politics, and why they finally put him out of the way as "the king of the Jews."

The kingdom was different, but not in the sense of church-state, soul-body, heaven-earth, eternity-time separa-

47

tion. The kingdom was spiritual, but it affected every national aspect of human existence. It was eternal and heavenly, but it injected itself into history and planted its feet firmly on the earth. It existed in the mind of God as a model and was, therefore, said to be a kingdom of heaven. But it also existed within the hearts and minds of those people who made room for it.

Those who embraced the kingdom of peace, love, and righteousness or opened their lives to it soon found that the kingdom within them wanted to get outside of them. That is, it wanted to spread until all the kingdoms of this world (family, village, synagogue, business, Judaism, the Roman empire) had become the kingdoms of our Christ. The kingdom became the disciple's transformation, his motivation, his passion, his vision.

Once it was inside of him, he had no need to establish a theology every time the salt and light of his witness confronted the rottenness and darkness of this world. The compulsions of the kingdom required no special defense. The compassion of the disciple did not have to be explained in every new situation. Love of God and man suddenly became a single command. Bringing the kingdom down to earth, from eternity into time, and from the inside out into the world was the most natural thing to do. The pietist-activist discussions and the differentiations between the social and personal gospels suddenly became irrelevant. What was revelant was that the kingdom had come and was coming, and that it was expanding.

Wherever it expanded, the political people inevitably complained that the heavenly kingdom was wrongly getting mixed up with politics. The business people too were upset and insisted that "business was business." But this did not stop the kingdom people, except some who invented a false doctrine of separations so that they could conveniently bypass the kingdoms of economics and politics in their proclamation.

Those who built bypass highways for the kingdom soon lost the kingdom blueprint itself. The kingdom just does not appear apart from people and outside of society. And the more they lost it, the more they identified with the prevailing religious and political tribalisms of the day. Thus, in the 1960s and 1970s, the kingdom was reduced to an unfinished American dream, just as in the 1930s it had become little more than a German Reich.

*　　*　　*

The foremost task of evangelism, therefore, is the recovery of the fulness of the vision represented by the kingdom. But even as I say this, I have a haunting fear that we will rush off to develop a new strategy which we think appropriate to the vision without really filling the vessels of evangelism with the substance of the new vision.

We have learned so well from the world of politics, entertainment, and commerce that we are now wordly specialists in strategy rather than God's specialists in substance. We have become experts in manipulating language and symbols so as to project favorable imagery that does not conform to reality, thereby brainwashing people with an escapist religion that immunizes them against the real thing.

Closely related to the ways of the world are the values of the world, and both are more a part of us than we realize. We have become so concerned with success and respectability, so wedded to society, so anxious to be the comforting chaplains of culture and the compromising priests of Presidents and Prime Ministers, that our potential role as God's true evangelists has become doubtful.

We are still evangelizing, of course, but mostly the defenders of the *status quo*, when, in fact, true evangelism should call forth the prophetic minority, the bearers of visions, the carriers of true revolution. We are still evangelizing, but as the somewhat deceptive and hard-sell insurance salesmen of yesterday have made the selling of insurance very difficult today, so also much of evangelism today is against evangelism tomorrow. The doors to China were closed as much by Christians as by Communists. And has it ever occurred to us how much we are closing all of Asia and Africa by our present, peculiarly American combination of cross, flag, and gun?

How can we get the vision that becomes a qualitative and permanent evangelism? All of the biblical visions arose from a profound dissatisfaction with the *status quo* and a very personal concern for society's total renewal. The biblical visionaries wanted the new order of the universal kingdom, of God's highest mountain, of the holy city coming out of heaven down to earth. The order was a revolutionary new one, not just stitches of an old one.

All of the above really boils down to a very simple message, one which we all have spoken once. We need only to ask now what it means. "Thy kingdom come, Thy will be done on earth as in heaven." If we discover its meaning and accept it for ourselves, we will have found a new evangelism, a true evangelism, the evangelism with an evangel, the evangelism that becomes the world's much needed revolution.

NOTES TO ESSAY IV

1. Harry Emerson Fosdick, *Christianity and Progress: The Cole Lectures for 1922* (New York: Revell, 1922), pp. 93-98.

2. Albert P. Blaustein and Robert L. Zangrando (ed.), *Civil Rights and the American Negro: A Documentary History* (New York: Trident, 1968), p. 10.

3. Quoted by Martin Luther King, Jr., in *The Christian Century*, October 8, 1958, p. 1141.

4. R. McGill, "Agony of a Southern Minister," *New York Times Magazine*, September 27, 1959, p. 17.

5. C. Kennan, "Church Leaders on School Segregation," *America*, July 10, 1954, p. 379.

6. Billy Graham, "The Unfinished Dream," *Christianity Today*, July 31, 1970, pp. 20-21.

7. Matthew 4:17-23. See also Matthew 6, 11, 13, 18; Mark 4, 10; Luke 11, 13, 18, 22.

V

The Law Above the Law of the Land

"Come, let us climb up to the mountain of the Lord . . . that he may teach us his ways."

—Isaiah 2:3

Every Sunday Christians gather together to celebrate the just society. The weekly worship of God arises from, consists of, and gives direction to daily concern for men's welfare. With the prophet Isaiah we believe that solemn assemblies and prayers are an abomination to the Lord if the worshipers do not "pursue justice and champion the oppressed, give the orphan his rights, plead the widow's cause" (Isaiah 1:12-17).

That pursuit of justice cannot proceed without reference to the laws of the land or to what we shall identify as the law above the law of the land. Examination of laws has always been a very involved process, and we must avoid the complicated exercises in legalism and literalism for which both lawyers and theologians have always had a fine reputation. Instead, we shall consider law in the broadest possible terms. Thus, we shall divide it into no more than two main categories: (1) the law that a land or nation is unto itself and (2) the laws that a nation has for itself. In the first instance we have law in the singular and in the second instance laws in the plural.

Perhaps these categories and their relationships to each other and to our theme can best be introduced by referring to other areas of life. Let me begin with a personal experience. Some little time ago one of my employers became interested in adding to my wages a fringe benefit in the form of an insurance policy. Insurance companies do not make such additions automatically, especially when the person to be insured has reached a certain age and achieved a certain shape.

In this instance, the insurance fringe could not be added without a medical inspection, which, among other things, required a trip to the cardiologist. The examining medical specialist took great care with the required readings, following the detailed instructions to the letter. Finally he became so angered by the company's excessive and irrelevant demands that he exclaimed: "Those insurance people are a law unto themselves!"

Insurance companies must not be singled out here to the neglect of other professions and interest groups. A Washington journalist has identified the lawyers in the District of Columbia as a powerful and exclusive kingdom.[1] History also provides examples of clergymen being a law unto themselves. The laboring class, too often abused and exploited, has in some unions achieved a sovereignty uniquely its own. The wealthy, always seemingly above the law, manage to bend almost every statute to their own advantage. It is a familiar scandal that hundreds of super-rich Americans manage not to pay a cent in taxes. And Canadian rich have been just as successful as their American counterparts in finding ways to cut the tax bill.[2] And, lest we exclude the lawmakers and administrators themselves, let us remember that notions of rulers ruling by divine right and power are still with us.

The law of the land is, of course, intended to be a law above the monopolies and sovereignties of the professions and special interest groups. The just nation develops laws for itself so that all its citizens may have equal rights with opportunities and justice for all. However, by seeking to be a superior law for all the members of a given society, that society, like the professions and power groups themselves, is likewise in danger of becoming a law unto itself. Such has been the case, more often than not, with nation-states.

*   *   *

The Law That a Nation Is Unto Itself. The evolutionary history of nation-states reminds us that they arose as a new and superior law, transcending the laws of a narrow tribalism, and of an oppressive feudal system, or more recently as a reaction to the exploitations of imperialism. The latter phenomenon has been observed particularly since World War II in the emergence of new nations from former colonial territories. For these once subordinate peoples, nationalism is definitely a law above the earlier colonial law of the land. For them it has meant moving on from political infancy to political adolescence on the road to political maturity. To quote Lubor J. Zink:

> Militant nationalism may still be the necessary formative ingredient in the recently decolonized parts of Asia and Africa. It may also be the only weapon that Soviet satellites have in their struggle for freedom. [3]

As far as Canada is concerned, however, Zink believes that nationalistic ferment of whatever description is a symptom of political regression. In expressing this opinion, he seems to overlook the fact that Canadian society, too, has the marks of colonialism and that a certain kind of nationalism might well be for Canadians a law above the present law of economic subservience and political dependence. On the other hand, to the extent that Canada is an independent nation, a chauvinistic nationalism is a return to social adolescence, if not to the principles of jungle law, rather than an advance to the higher international law of world community and federalism.

That such regression is a real possibility for Canada is attested to by the history books, which suggest that the struggle to destroy the law of state sovereignty may take even longer than the battle against the doctrine of the divine right of kings. Two world wars and the two international organizations they produced were intended to end forever the nationalistic exclusiveness that caused those wars. But jingoistic and idolatrous patriotism has by no means come to an end. Today the lower law of "national interest" and the "national commitment" has some frightening manifestations in countries like the USSR and the USA. The tragedy is not only that the citizens of those nations must themselves live under a nationalism that has become a law unto itself, but also that they must become a part of the extension of that law to other societies—whether Czechoslovakia, Vietnam, or Canada. And such an extension is a return to the imperialism, colonialism, and feudalism of an earlier day.

Once the law of nationalism has been accepted by a society as its highest law, it will justify the killing of any number of thousands of people, the drafting of any number of millions of men, the waste of any quantity of human and material resources, the expenditure of any number of billions of dollars, the violation of any international law, and the distortion of any truth to satisfy its purposes and to achieve its ends. So holy and divine can the law of nationalism become that the burning of babies to defend it is a lesser crime than the burning of draft cards to defy it!

The draft-card burners, conscientious objectors, and protesters in general are being blamed for national lawlessness and disorder, when in fact it is the nation which, measured by the higher law, is the greatest lawbreaker and perpetrator of disorder. The occupation of buildings by students is 'peanuts' compared to the occupation of whole countries by armies. To be sure, when dissenters become anarchists, a law unto themselves, they are following a lower law, but a goodly number are simply obeying the law above the law of the land. While they too are loosely called anarchists, they are really prophets, whose children and historians will some day rise up and call them blessed.

The law of nationalism, however, does not readily accept dissent, not even in a democracy, and Martin Luther King is not the only one to have suffered the consequences of raising his prophetic voice against this jungle law. With him and before him there have been others, like Dietrich Bonhoeffer in the Third Reich and the Quakers and Anabaptists of Europe and America.

As a Mennonite, I am proud to belong to a group of people who have insisted for 450 years that the international law of God, written in the hearts of men and in nature, is a higher law than the laws of tribalism, racism, or nationalism. We remember with gratitude those many martyrs who died rather than bow down to church and state authorities who were playing God. Foremost among them

was Jesus of Nazareth, whose protest won him the deroga-
tory, but correct, title of king, his challenge to false
authority having been the main cause of his execution.

We are deeply grateful that in countries like Canada the
law of conscience was recognized and that when we refused to take up arms against our fellowmen, the law
nonetheless made allowance for what we believed was the
law of God. It gives us no little concern, therefore, when
we see how much Canada is now in danger of acquiescing
to the law of an external nationalism and placing that law
above the conscience of those men who will not, and
should not, be told to hate and kill, and who seek refuge
from induction or incarceration.

The words of William Blackstone, spoken two hundred
years ago as he commented on the laws of England, still
apply today:

> Man, considered as a creature, must necessarily be subject to
> the laws of his creator. . . . This law of nature, being co-equal
> with mankind, and dictated by God himself, is of course
> superior in obligation to any other. It is binding over all the
> globe, in all countries, and at all times: no human laws are of
> any validity, if contrary to this: and such of them as are valid
> derive all their force, and all their authority, mediately or
> immediately, from this original.[4]

The Prophet Isaiah had an exciting vision of the nations
of the world reaching for this higher law and also some
beautiful words (2:2-3) to describe it. He saw the mountain of the house of the Lord becoming a hill higher than
all the hills in the land, higher even than Parliament Hill
and Capitol Hill. In his vision the peoples of the world
were flowing to that hill to learn the ways of the Lord and
to walk in his paths. Some have seen the fulfilment of this
vision in the United Nations and world federalism. We see
it there, at least in part, but the highest hill rises much
higher than the UN. John of Patmos puts it this way: "By
its light [the glory of God] shall the nations walk; and the
kings of the earth shall bring their glory unto it . . . and
there shall be no night there . . . " (Revelation 21:22-25).

*   *   *

The Laws That a Nation Has for Itself. A nation can

go against the higher law not only as a law *unto* itself, but also when it makes laws *for* itself. In this latter area we have a paradox, because the nation that may be most unwilling to accept a higher law for itself nonetheless promotes one among its citizens. They are told that as individuals or as special interest groups they cannot, or may not, be a law unto themselves. They are entitled, so they are told, to rights, but not to such rights as would violate the rights of others or challenge state sovereignty.

Laws are formulated from time to time, supposedly to insure the rights of all and the power of the state. According to the lawmakers, the statutes passed at a given time represent the highest insights of a society and its rulers at that time. Another historical opinion, however, says that a nation's laws are determined not so much by the highest insights of a society as by the selfish interest of the strongest people in that society. As one observer has said: "Law is merely the expression of the will of the strongest for the time being, and therefore laws have no fixity, but shift from generation to generation."[5]

Power structures change, but so do the insights of a society, often with changing situations. Thus it happens that laws become irrelevant and ineffectual. Yet it is not always easy to get the written laws unwritten, because the law of the land often achieves the status of a divine law not to be meddled with. The strength of a law once written explains why Canada's Criminal Code had not been retouched in a major way for nearly eighty years when the so-called Bill C-150 received third reading in the House of Commons in 1969. The law's resistance to change made it refreshing to hear the Justice Minister say, in introducing the omnibus bill, that law reform should be continuous:

> There is nothing immutable or unchangeable about the criminal law in this country. There is nothing infallible about parliament which enacts it. Reform of the criminal law should not be just a decennial tradition—not just once in ten years. I think reform of the criminal law should take place more frequently than even just once each parliament. . . . Today all of us here embark upon that endless search for justice and for an understanding and compassionate system of law, perhaps falling short of the goal in our uncertain stumblings, but always seeking the ultimate reach of the human heart. [6]

By that statement and his announced program, the Minister of Justice clearly indicated that the law of the land, while it must be the law for a given time, is not necessarily the law of the land for all time. There is a law above that law. The higher law may at a given time not be within spiritual reach or political grasp, but it is there nonetheless waiting for us, and we must strive to find it, to formulate it, and to follow it. The just society is not something that arrives one day and is with us forever. Like the kingdom of God, it is always coming, though in our hearts and in our dreams it is already present.

Whether the bill in question did in all its clauses bring the law of the land to a higher level is, of course, an open issue. Extended debate demonstrated that there was considerable disagreement in certain areas. We must expect that the last word on these issues has not yet been spoken. And, as the Minister of Justice said: "If in the light of experience any changes or additions to the Criminal Code appear not to have been in the public interest, they can always be changed or repealed at any time."[7]

It has often been said—especially by people disagreeing with proposed legal reforms—that it is impossible to legislate morality. If they mean that an unwilling heart cannot be made moral even if an external conformity is enforced, they are right, of course. But they should not overlook the fact that the law not only reflects the conscience of a society but it also informs it. Besides being an instrument of order, law is a powerful medium of education.

It has been said, and with good evidence, that the Supreme Court of the United States has been a revolutionary committee in recent years. Its rulings on civil rights since 1954, for instance, have effected widespread social changes in the country. Not least of all, these decisions have helped many religious people read their holy books in a new context, only to discover that revelation is not against racial integration after all.

So the law is an instrument of education, of change, of revolution, as it is also the tool of order and of justice. Sometimes the law is, like John the Baptist, a forerunner for the spirit, like that of Jesus. Indeed, good laws, like the laws of Moses, are a schoolmaster unto Christ.

There is yet another question raised by the issue of law

reform. Are the laws being formulated really relevant to the big problems hurting the country and the really basic issues confronting society? We have already seen that the law has often been the instrument of powerful groups to control all the "criminal" elements in society—meaning all those in any way opposed to the powerful. So there have been many laws and punishments for the weak and their little crimes and few for the powerful and their big crimes. To this day little thieves get thrown into jail, while some big thieves are elevated to positions of power.

In some areas of life, our society is not advancing very rapidly beyond the primitive laws of the jungle. One of these has to do with the laws governing the relationships of people and property. The law above the law of the land says that all the resources of this world were meant for all the people. But the prevailing law of the land says that whatever you can lay hold of by military, legal, or financial power is yours to have in perpetuity, to do with as you please, whether you need it or not, and even if such ownership hurts others. Such law is behind the times, behind the conscience of the mass of humanity, and below the higher law. It represents less insight than the laws of Moses given in the desert and in a rather primitive culture. Already by the laws of over three millennia ago, property was tied to stewardship and benefits for all the people. There was no such thing as perpetual ownership to meet the nonexistent needs of the few at the expense of the real needs of the many.

The just society has, however, come nowhere near bringing justice to this big problem area. Measured by the property laws that are higher than the laws of the jungle, we of the West stand condemned. Our polluted soil, water, and air are witness to the fact that we are robbing our children. The familiar commentary that the rich are getting richer while the poor are getting poorer is evidence that the few are robbing the many.

It is often said in our society that the rich get richer because they work harder, save more, and generally are more virtuous, while the poor don't get ahead because they are either lazy, or foolish, or wasteful. All of these factors may enter into the picture, but they are by no means the only factors. A very significant part of the problem lies in our written and unwritten laws that sanction and encourage the profiteering of the few at the expense of the many, laws that subsidize the rich with oil depletion allowances and unlimited capital gains concessions, but which put the poor on humiliating welfare allowances as the only way to get their daily bread.

Our nation has always held that the air waves are public property, not to be abused and exploited by private profiteers at the public expense. The Canadian Radio and Television Commission has been reinforcing this higher law by calling broadcasters to give an accounting of their performance and to justify why their ownership of a given frequency should be continued. This is a step in the right direction. But when will we realize that land, air, water, and oil are also a public trust meant to bless and prosper all the people equally? A higher law than the laws of our land is calling for a new relationship between all the property and all the people!

*   *   *

After suggesting laws that are higher than nationalism and mammonism, I can hear someone saying: how do you know, how does anybody know, which laws are of a lower or of a higher order? It is a fair question, and we must address ourselves to it briefly before we conclude.

The simplest answer might be the traditional Christian response: the higher law is revealed to us by God in the Bible and through Jesus Christ. And in a way, this is what I would like to say, because I believe it. In the same way that some people see the highest law in Moses or Marx, I see it in Jesus of Nazareth. But I also know that in the final analysis the Bible and Christ say to people and to a nation what people want them to say. It is only too true that jingoistic nationalists, ruthless capitalists, and rabid racists have made Christ over into their own image and quoted the Bible in support of their own selfish laws.

We must, therefore, seek another approach, and I believe both history and theology give us a clue. As we look back we discover that higher law emerged or was rediscovered whenever and wherever the poor and the oppressed struggled to be free, or where men and women who were free wrestled on behalf of the oppressed.

The moral law of Moses, remember, came out of a 400-year enslavement in Egypt, and Jesus brought an even higher law, when as a carpenter's son of questionable legitimacy and birth he arose as a spokesman for the downtrodden. Remember his inaugural address in the synagogue of Nazareth:

> The Spirit of the Lord is upon me because he has anointed me; he has sent me to announce good news to the poor, to proclaim release for prisoners and recovery of sight for the blind; to let the broken victims go free, to proclaim the year of the Lord's favor (Luke 4:18-19).

Whenever the powerful and the privileged were humble and wise enough to listen to the spokesmen for the poor and weak—those spokesmen were the prophets of God—peaceful reform became possible. But where they resisted, the higher law broke through eventually anyway, though regrettably by way of a bloody detour. All of history and the best of theology agree with the late President Kennedy's remark that "Those who make peaceful revolution impossible, will make violent revolution inevitable."[8]

All of the above means that if Canadian and American society is to move continuously toward the higher law there will have to be some turning in new directions for the source of that law. It is, for instance, inconceivable that a newer and better Indian Act should be written without the help of the Indians. Similarly, it is impossible to achieve justice in housing without a greater voice on the part of those who feel the crisis most.

And the just society is a contradiction in terms if in that society the rich will be most influential in the writing of property and tax laws. Indeed, I would go so far as to say that a higher law for our penal system can emerge only if we give some ear also to the prisoners themselves. And our welfare programs may not be determined only by the welfare bosses.

As far as the nation as a law in itself is concerned, it is the weakness of our democracy that foreign policy in Canada, as in the USA and other idolatrous states, is of all questions the least debatable. Not only must the citizenry of a nation submit itself in patriotic compliance, but the masses outside, so much affected by these policies, are rarely heard, not even in the counsels of the U.N.

That is why the most urgent need of the would-be just society is courageous spokesmen at all levels on behalf of those who cannot speak for themselves but who should be spoken for. Those unheard voices and unrecognized messages are an indispensable source for the higher law. They are for our society a vital part of the voice of God. Such spokesmen, of course, have a most difficult task, for every higher law is in its beginnings always a minority position. But no law reform ever becomes politically possible until some minority spokesman has made it morally necessary. Before the politician can stick out his neck, a prophet must often lay down his life.

Most of us are tempted always to be with the safe majority, but in Christianity—and also in a democracy—all of us are called to be prophetic minorities. This holds true for the loyal opposition in the House, but also for the loyal opposition in the hustings. It applies to lawyers and theologians, but also to civil servants and church members. A just society comes, and a higher law takes hold, only as we all do our parts, beginning of course in our own hearts.

NOTES TO ESSAY V

1. Ronald Goldfarb, "A Fifth Estate—Washington Lawyers," *New York Times Magazine*, May 5, 1968, p. 37.

2. Douglas H. Fullerton, "Rich Using Great Skill to Avoid Tax," *Ottawa Citizen*, April 26, 1969, p. 8.

3. Lubor J. Zink, "Nationalism Perpetuates Jungle Law," *Toronto Telegram*, March 3, 1969, p. 7.

4. Blackstone, *Commentaries on the Law of England* (1765).

5. Brooks Adams, *The Law of Civilization and Decay*.

6. Hon. John W. Turner, "Opening Speech on Criminal Law Reform," *House of Commons Debates*, January 23, 1969, pp. 10-11.

7. *Ibid.*

8. Inaugural address, January 20, 1960.

VI

The Christian Response to
National Disorder

> *"Every person must submit to the . . . authorities. . . ."*   —Romans 13:1

> *"We must obey God rather than men."* —Acts 5:29

The title of this essay identifies two aspects of the problem at hand: a theological dimension called "Christian response" and a sociological situation referred to as "national disorder." One might assume that the sociological situation has been adequately defined and clarified by the law-and-order politicians and that we are now free to discuss our disagreements on the proper Christian response, to engage in the theological hair-splitting for which churchmen are noted and which has given them so much fun—while at the same time providing them with a livelihood! Such assumptions are not justified.

In the first place, the meaning of national disorder has not been clarified. It means different things to different people. To illustrate, it means one thing to the Federal Bureau of Investigation, which sees a great jump in violent crime in the United States in recent years, and quite another thing to Karl Menninger of the Topeka Menninger Foundation, who says that "violent crime has been diminishing all the time."[1] And the otherwise excellent 1968 *Report of the National Advisory Commission on Civil Disorders* treated national disorders only in a limited way.

Second, true theological understanding is impossible without some relation to a sociological setting about which one is adequately informed. While it is true that "in the beginning was the (theological) word," it is also true that "this word became (sociological) flesh." It is important for us, therefore, to look at the flesh in history and in contemporary society and then relate the word to it. The proper Christian response to national disorder begins with an understanding of that disorder.

Most of this essay will be an identification of various types of national disorder, relating them to each other and differentiating among them, indicating in each instance the nature of the Christian response.

*   *   *

First, national disorder is brought about by prophets and the prophetic community, all those bold witnesses and loyal servants whose life goal is to make all the national orders (or kingdoms) to become the international order (or kingdom) of our Christ, who alone will reign forever. A survey of history reveals a host of these prophets, dating back to Moses, who upset the national order of the pharaohs by staging huge demonstrations, withdrawing the labor force, and then "blowing up the bridge" precisely when the National Guard was crossing the Red Sea in hot pursuit.

R. R. Palmer reports how the third-century Roman Empire was blaming all of its national disorders on the Christians, subjecting them to wholesale persecution. The Christians were not actually disorderly, but with their entirely new sense of human values "they protested against the massacre of prisoners of war, against the mistreatment and degradation of slaves, against the sending of gladiators to kill each other in the arena of another's leisure."[2] Palmer continues:

> It was for their political ideas that the Christians were most often denounced and persecuted. The Roman Empire was a world state; there was no other state but it; no living human being except the Emperor was sovereign; no one anywhere on earth was his equal. . . . A cult of Caesar was established, regarded as necessary to maintain the state which was the world itself. All this the Christians firmly refused to accept. It

63

was because they would not worship Caesar that the Roman officials regarded them as monstrous social incendiaries who must be persecuted and stamped out.[3]

The national disorder for which the Christians were responsible was the subjugation of the national order to the higher order of God, a subjugation the so-called sovereign could not accept because he wished himself to be regarded as God. However, the Christians did not disregard him completely. While they did not accept him for what he pretended to be, they did accept him for what he was, and they followed the instructions of Paul to "be subject to the governing authorities" (Romans 13:1-7).

Social order was important to them, as were the instruments of that order. If they were anarchists—as the emperor said they were—they were anarchists not in the sense that they recognized no authority but themselves, but in the sense that they recognized beyond the imperial authority a higher authority. Like Paul, they placed a premium on obedience to the state, for they took his Romans 13 seriously; but they placed an even higher premium on obedience to God, which is the reason that so many of them, like Paul, were put to death by the Caesar. So, while they were guilty of a certain disorder, we should not forget the contribution they made to order. As Justin has said of his time (the second century): "The world lives from the prayers of the Christians and from the obedience of the Christians to the law of the state."[4]

While the first-, second-, and third-century Christians have thus left us an example of how to promote the national order while at the same time disturbing it, they are by no means the only ones. A careful search reveals their type in almost every culture and generation. Not least we discover them in the Protestant Reformation, in which the Anabaptists, above all others, discovered what it meant to test the national order by the demands of Christ's international kingdom.

Popular historians have referred to their teaching as "the separation of church and state," but if separation then would have meant what we presume it to mean now, they would not have been seen as such a threat and so many thousands would not have had to pay for separation with their lives. For them separation meant sensitivity to the state playing God and a prophetic witness against any imperial claims to sovereignty. That is why they, too, were disturbers of the national orders of their time.[5]

* * *

A closely related national disorder is that arising from the emperors and sovereigns and their patriotic subjects. Patriotism has two sides to it. As William R. Inge has said: "Patriotism varies from a noble devotion to a moral lunacy."[6] More often than not, it has been the latter, a kind of religion, or to quote Guy de Maupassant, "the eggs from which wars are hatched."[7]

Super-patriotism is in our time what emperor worship was in the days of the Roman Empire. While it does not venerate presidents and kings as gods, it has its own idolatries and its idolatrous symbols. While it no longer speaks of the divine right of kings, it acts out the divine right of states. In times past, super-patriotism demanded of the British that they help Britannia always to "rule the waves," and of the Germans that they place Germany above all else in the world. Today it requires Russians to march on foreign soil and trample on the rights of Czechoslovakians, so that their own national power is not endangered. It forces Americans to go 10,000 miles away to make unsafe any number of Asian villages in order, allegedly, to make safe the streets of San Francisco.

While the super-patriots thus become the champions of the national order, they are in fact the ones most disruptive of the national order. The greatest anarchists of our time are not those who take the law into their own hands in the streets, but those who take the law into their hands on the seas everywhere, on the land everywhere, and in the sky everywhere, who flout every human law, every international law, every divine law in the name of what is called national security.

* * *

George Jean Nathan has identified a third cause of national disorder by suggesting that "patriotism is often an arbitrary veneration of real estate above principles."[8] If the veneration for property, which in our society also spells power and privilege, were only a vague feeling, our problem might not be as acute, but it has, more often than not, become a law.

As an unwritten law it has become the value system by which a society operates and as a written law it has become the basis for judgment of what is criminal and what is not. So it happens that the ghetto blacks who loot the neighborhood stores are identified as criminal, while the bosses and merchants who have been exploiting the poor and the weak for years are good citizens. Yet, we might well ask whether all the Negroes of all time in America have stolen, burned, or looted as much of the white man's property as the white man has taken from the Negro in unpaid wages. In any event, it is most certainly a fact that the Negro has not yet offended against the white man's property as much as the white man has offended against the Negro or Indian person. Yet, the Negroes and the Indians, the poor and the weak and the underprivileged, are the ones that are confronted with responsibility for national disorder, when in fact the responsibility lies with the privileged and the powerful. As the Kerner Commission said:

> White racism is essentially responsible for the explosive mixture which has been accumulating in our cities since the end of World War II. Among the ingredients of this mixture are pervasive discrimination and segregation in employment, education and housing, which have resulted in the continuing exclusion of great numbers of Negroes from the benefits of economic progress.[9]

What should be the Christian response to this situation? Russian history tells us what it should not be. At the time when Western Europe was being prepared for the Protestant Reformation there was a great debate in the Russian Orthodox Church between the so-called non-possessors and the possessors.

The non-possessors denied ecclesiastical power, landed wealth, privilege, and the protection of the state, while the possessors made all of these of fundamental importance.[10] The possessors won the debate and thus gave the Russian church and aristocracy the ideological foundation that undergirded a most unjust society, which eventually ripened for revolution. That great national disorder, the Russian Revolution, has been blamed on Lenin and the Bolsheviks. In fact its seeds were planted by the possessors—the powerful and the privileged in the religious Russian society. Revolutionary ferment was in evidence in Russia throughout the nineteenth century, and many there were who protested the unjust social conditions, but the powerful and the privileged always managed to put them down as disrupters of the national order. Affluent twentieth-century society is not too much different from nineteenth-century Russia.

* * *

The fourth type of national disorder is that brought about by the new protesters. It goes without saying that contemporary protest movements have both positive and negative aspects. We shall, for the present, amplify the positive.

In the popular mind, nurtured by the law-and-order people, much national disorder would vanish if only the protesters would disappear. Indeed, in not a few places the protesters themselves have been identified with the criminal element. The distinction between crime and protest is needed as much in America today as it was in ancient Rome and in nineteenth-century Russia.

Former US Supreme Court Justice Abe Fortas has made an eloquent defense of dissent and protest as the desired "alternative to violence," but he also defines the limits of such protest, obligated as he is to defend the law as defined by the Constitution and the Supreme Court, beyond which for him there is no higher authority.[11] So Fortas is bound by the same reasoning that prescribes the order of the super-patriots. The protesters, on the other hand, often have caught a vision of justice that goes beyond the laws of the Constitution, the President, and the Supreme Court. They have this in common with the prophetic Christian community. The Supreme Court is concerned about legality, while the protesters are often concerned about a morality that transcends and/or offends legality.

67

Many protesters are motivated by lesser laws. But many of them are the secular prophets of our day, and they should find in the Christian community a sympathetic response to their diagnosis of the national ills. To blame them for the national disorder is like mistaking the doctor for the disease.

The protest movement has an element in common with the democratic process we call politics. We must, in the fifth place, speak about the national disorder produced by the politicians.

* * *

Democracy itself is a type of national disorder, which, with all its discomforts and irregularities, we have accepted as essential to the protection of other values that we hold to be important. This disorder of democracy reaches its peak during a political campaign. I venture to guess that seldom in the US is more offensive language used, more disrespect for men in high places shown, more stunts pulled to get publicity, more signs paraded, more streets littered, more grass trampled, and more time wasted than in an election campaign.

All of this disorder is tolerated. Quite properly, I think. But why can the tolerance not be extended to the times between election campaigns, when lesser politicians, the secular protesters and the religious prophets, continue the democratic process, while they speak for transcendent loyalties, for unpopular causes, for unrepresented people, and for the forgotten God? Even the universities could avert much physical disorder on campus if they would risk in time the disorder of student involvement in the democratic process.

The true democrats of our day speak the word of truth not only in the season of the socially accepted campaign, but also out of season. Though this results in a certain amount of disorder, the Christian welcomes it as a necessary ingredient of the ongoing revolution. He also reserves for himself the right to speak even when what he has to say does not fit the recognized social etiquette or the entrenched political establishment.

68

A sixth source of social disorder is the enforcers of social order. The Christian recognizes the need for such officials, of course, inasmuch as he believes in social discipline and moral judgment. But the agents of this discipline and judgment are not to be accepted unconditionally. They are subject to standards of legality and morality.

Some progress has been made in the field of penology in recent years, but the laws and methods governing the enforcement of law and order and the punishment of criminals are in many instances themselves part of the social disorder. While politicians parade around advocating the enforcement of law and order, the nation's prisons themselves remain criminal, with the worst of them practicing "old-fashioned barbarity."[12]

And—lest Canadians wash their hands—in our own national capital, within a stone's throw of a $40 million new arts center, a jail was discovered, the highest occupancy provincial jail, that was little more than a medieval castle, with cells only two inches wider than a single cot, cells without windows, without electric lights, and without toilets.

Our Lord told us that in the final judgment we would not be judged by the number of criminals we had caught or how successfully we had incarcerated them, but that we would stand or fall according to how we had treated the prisoners (Matthew 25:31-46). One of the Christian responses to national disorder, therefore, is to bring some moral sense and humane law to bear on the instruments of order. A vast assignment in reform awaits the makers, administrators, interpreters, enforcers, and supporters of our laws.

The common reaction of a criminal society, however, is to wash its hands by catching more individual "criminals" and making them the scapegoats of the social disorder of which society itself is a part. The policeman—God help him, his lot is not a happy one!—is placed in the awkward position of helping society to wash its hands. As social disorder increases, society does not call for reform but rather for more rigorous enforcement of existing laws. Inasmuch as more of these laws have been made for the powerful and privileged than for the underrepresented and weak, the police are forced to act out the wishes of the powerful. The result is an increasing emphasis on police power, on a more effective police technology, both of which together lead to the police state.

The police-state mentality, reinforced by the new technology, believes that more police are the answer to any and every social disorder. History gives evidence, however, that the police themselves can be a central cause of social disorder. It would be grossly unfair, of course, to generalize and blame the police for all ghetto disturbances, but it does illustrate one aspect of the national disorder problem. Many police in our country are gentlemen who remain calm and restrained in spite of great danger and provocation. They see their role not as protecting their power and security but as making every contribution, at great personal risk and sacrifice, to keep order and peace in a community. To them we take off our hats and offer our support. This is the kind of police that is a real contribution to social order. We need many more of them to replace those who, with poor social attitudes, inferior education, and weak understanding of the causes of social unrest, proudly parade the physical symbols of their power, and generally act as though society was made for the police, not police for society.

*　　*　　*

Finally, we identify a seventh dimension of the social disorder scene, the criminal aspect. We place this last and emphasize it the least, not because it is a minor problem, but because the so-called criminal element has been made to carry from time immemorial almost the entire disorder burden of society. These are the people who are blamed for everything. They go to jail not only for themselves but for all the shortcomings of the politicians, all the sins of the powerful and privileged, and almost all the failings of the police.

There are criminals, of course, but their number is considerably less than certain law-and-order people would have us believe, for they make little allowance for genuine prophets or for the new protestants, or even for lesser politicians who speak out of season. They also fail to differentiate between those who break the laws of man only while obeying God, and those who break the laws of both man and God. What is legal and what is moral are not always identical. Many of God's men, including such early saints as the Apostle Paul and such latter-day saints as Martin Luther King, Jr., have been in jail for civil disobedience, for breaking the laws of men, while attending to the business of the Lord.

The collective shape of the criminal element needs to be redefined. We must include not only those who are weak and poor and defenseless, but also those who are the powerful and the privileged, not only the petty thieves but the big exploiters, not only the abusers of property but also the abusers of people, not only the blue-collar criminals, but also the white-collar criminals, not only those in the ghettos but also those in the high places.

Then, when we have reviewed what all must properly be identified as criminal, we can proceed to deal with the criminal element, and deal with it we must. There is a place for social discipline; there is a place for legal and moral judgment; there is a place for punishment; and there is a place for the use of physical force (though, according to my understanding of the Christian revelation, there is no place for capital punishment).

There is also no place for punishment just for the sake of punishment and for the sake of satisfying a punishment-oriented, vengeance-filled society. All punishment must have a redemptive purpose, seeking the restoration of the offender to society. If this purpose could be brought to the top in all our penology, there surely would be widespread reform.

*   *   *

The Christian response to national disorder calls for reform and attention to those causes of disorder that we have most often overlooked—the injustices of our laws and law enforcement institutions and procedures; the social, economic, and political injustices of society experienced by many of the poor, weak, and underrepresented people; the abuses of power and privilege; the crimes of super-patriotism and super-nationalism, arising from nations and rulers that are laws unto themselves.

In short, the Christian response to national disorder in our time calls for the prophetic word and deed directed at those in high places, the church included, and the sympathetic, understanding, and redeeming word and deed to those in places we have described as being low. And so, I close with the words of Ogden Nash:

> *Gentlemen of the High Command,*
> *Who crucify the slums,*
> *There was an earlier Golgotha;*
> *The Third day comes.* [13]

NOTES TO ESSAY VI

1. "Violent Crime Is Decreasing," *The Globe and Mail* (Toronto), October 30, 1968, p. 3.

2. R. R. Palmer. *A History of the Modern World* (New York: Knopf, 1959), p. 11.

3. *Ibid.*, p. 12.

4. Quoted in Paul Tillich, *A Complete History of Christian Thought* (New York: Harper, 1968), p. 29.

5. Frank H. Epp, *The Glory and the Shame* (Winnipeg: Canadian Mennonite Publishing Association, 1968), pp. 41-49.

6. Quoted in George Seldes, *The Great Quotations* (New York: Simon and Schuster, 1967), p. 716.

7. *Ibid.*, p. 717.

8. *Ibid.*

9. "Summary of the Report of the National Advisory Commission on Civil Disorders," *NCC Information Service*, March 1968, p. 5.

10. Nicholas V. Riasanovsky, *A History of Russia* (New York: Oxford, 1963), pp. 135-137.

11. Abe Fortas, *Concerning Dissent and Civil Disobedience* (New York: New American Library, 1968).

12. Bruce Jackson, "Our Prisons Are Criminal," *New York Times Magazine*, September 22, 1968, p. 42.

13. Quoted in *Masterpieces of Religious Verse* (New York: Harper, 1948), p. 472.

VII

American Causes of World War III

There is a growing belief that America is no longer the historic America, that it is a bastard empire which relies on superior force to achieve its purpose, and is no longer providing an example to the wisdom and humanity of a free society.
—Walter Lippmann, 1967

It should be made clear from the outset that the topic of this essay is not meant to imply American causes only. Such a position would represent an oversimplification of the international situation and, as an analysis, would be both unfair and untrue. There are Asian, African, and European causes. There are, in all probability, Chinese and Soviet causes. There could once more be French, German, and British causes. And there are causes which must be defined not in continental and national ways, but in human social, economic, and religious terms. Essays could, and should, be written on all of these.

Yet there are American causes, and they should be brought to our attention. These causes have, for reasons I will shortly submit, become the most fundamental and primary causes. Besides, they are the ones closest to home, the ones we can do most about, and the ones we are obligated to do something about if we would escape the judgments of history and our children.

The causes of world war have often been identified with

specific events, such as the war in Vietnam, or with specific individuals, such as a given President. Events and individuals are usually the precipitating factors and they become the causal symbols of a war, but to focus on these would be too superficial. There are deeper problems and graver causes confronting us and pointing to World War III even if there were no Vietnam.

The deeper causes lie with a great shift in modes of thinking and feeling and patterns of acting in American society, a shift from those values making for peace and those contributing to war. This change should not be seen in absolute terms as though America was once completely good and is now completely bad. On the contrary, the American character, like that of any society, has always been ambivalent and probably always will be. Perhaps the observable change is not so much a shift in character as the recent accentuation of a set of negative values that always were there.

That there has been a change is, of course, acknowledged by many individuals, although it is variously interpreted and described. Already in his 1968 State of the Union message, the late President Johnson spoke about "a certain restlessness—a questioning" that had come over the country. His successor in office, Richard Nixon, identified the problem as "a crisis of spirit" as he launched his campaign. Senator J. W. Fulbright claimed that "the Great Society has become a sick society" and that "America, which only a few years ago seemed to the world to be a model of democracy and social justice, has become a symbol of violence and undisciplined power."[1]

If these appraisals of the situation are true, and more and more people are concluding that they are, what precisely has been happening? What is the nature of the change that has brought about this restlessness, this crisis, this sickness, and unfortunately, the probable causes of World War III? Let me suggest several possibilities.

* * *

First of all, America's worldwide philanthropy has turned into unprecedented imperial profiteering. Again, the shift is not absolute. There has always been in America both diligence in making money and generosity in giving it away. The Andrew Carnegies and John D. Rockefellers are some of the best symbols of both money-making and money-sharing. Both men were multi-millionaires; both were also determined philanthropists who together distributed a billion dollars to worthwhile causes. What these men have done in a big way millions of Americans have done in lesser ways. Annually they put no less than eight billion dollars into the coffers of their favorite charities.

The gifts of America's generous citizens have been more than matched by the collective action of voluntary and governmental agencies. Recall the work of the United States Food Administration, which after 1917 fed war-torn Europe, the American Relief Administration, which after 1920 fed much of Russia, and the Marshall Plan, which from 1948-51 provided over $10 billion for food, machinery, and other products to Europe. During the 1966 famine in India the USA organized the largest peace-time armada ever to be assembled in world history, and no less than 600 ships delivered nine million tons of American surplus food to India.[2]

Even in Vietnam at the height of the war there was evidence of this philanthropic thrust, although the late David Lawrence of *US News and World Report* definitely overstated the case when he called

> what the United States is doing in Vietnam . . . the most significant example of philanthropy extended by one people to another that we have witnessed in our times. . . . The whole world must inevitably recognize the American effort as completely devoid of any selfish or material interest.[3]

Philanthropy is, however, only one of the motives of the American soul. If the profit motive has not always been dominant, it certainly has become that in recent years, as manifested in individual practice and collective policy both at home and abroad. The beginnings of American involvement in Vietnam already during the French period were related to economic profit. This is clearly stated in the late President Eisenhower's memoirs, where he gives as one reason for assisting France: "On the material side, it would have spelled the loss of valuable deposits of tin and prodigious supplies of rubber and rice. . . ."[4]

Economic interest in Vietnam was not an isolated phenomenon, but rather a fractional example of a world-wide policy, spearheaded by the big American corporations and supported by the United States government. A modest foreign investment of $8.4 billion in 1945 had by the end of 1967 increased nearly eight times, to over $64 billion.

Although only six percent of the world's people, Americans now control nearly sixty percent of its natural resources and enjoy more than forty percent of its total income. *Time* magazine refers to this overseas investment as "the globalization of American business."[5] Another magazine reported:

> It's rare nowadays for more than a month or two to pass without an American bank's disclosure that it is starting or expanding operations overseas. Fifty-four U.S. Banks are represented in 104 countries . . . 26 more banks than were listed two years ago.[6]

Sometimes America's massive foreign aid program is cited as an example of the philanthropic motive, and well it might be. But when it is remembered that during all this time the richest nation has been getting richer, that of $61.3 billion given in aid since 1953 to the developing regions, $16.5 billion was military aid, that only $39.5 billion were outright grants, and that much of the total came back through the compulsory purchase of American products, the philanthropic element shrinks considerably.[7]

When the dependent nations come to the conclusion that self-determination is more important to them than foreign capital, which tends to dominate them, they move in various ways to overcome their problem. Some countries, like Canada, seek peaceful and evolutionary means, while other societies, like Cuba, turn to violence and revolution. More and more of the poor peoples of the world are coming to the conclusion that the only way to achieve their sovereignty is to seize it, for a dominant empire rarely surrenders control voluntarily.

The rich man, whether he knows it or not, is actually harassed by two types of insecurity. On the one hand is the external threat from the poor, the Robin Hoods, the would-be Robin Hoods, and other empire builders. On the other hand is the unrecognized internal guilty feeling of the rich man that he has more than his share. This feeling in turn causes him to imagine "thieves" without, and these become as terrifying to him as though they were real. In his dreams his dominoes are always falling. His conscience speaks to him but to him it is nothing but Communist propaganda. Since he cannot differentiate between his subjective fears and the objective threat he has only one way of reacting. He becomes his own Sheriff of Nottingham—thereby compounding one cause for conflict with another.

* * *

This introduces a second major change in America, a shift from at least a degree of pacifism in her value system to a monstrous militarism, unprecedented in her history and that of the whole world.

Some of my Quaker friends have challenged the thesis that there has been, and still is, a significant pacifism in America. In their opinion, the nation has always been warlike, and they point to the Indian wars, the War of Independence, the War of 1812, the Mexican War, the Civil War, the Spanish-American War, the World Wars, the Korean War, and the Vietnam War as evidence. They remind us that since 1776 the US Army has filched more square miles (over three million) of earth by sheer military conquest than any other army in the world, except that of Great Britain. Robert Leckie makes a similar point:

> In American folklore the myth of "the most peace-loving nation in the world" still persists. But the fact is that American history is not only concurrent with the annals of American arms, but is as firmly woven into it as a strand of rope. . . . By war the Americans learned to organize and rule themselves. . . . It has been by war more than by peace that our institutions have been proclaimed and defended, our industries developed, our culture enriched, our history made national, our arts and our sciences improved. . . .[8]

Yet, all the wars that have been fought have also been disapproved by a sizeable segment of the population. Even

77

the War of Independence was flatly opposed by a large number of American settlers, and at least 40,000 migrated to Canada. A pacifist stance kept America out of both world wars at least for a time, and it is estimated that between the wars perhaps as many as twelve million Americans were members or adherents of the peace movement.[9]

America's leaders promoted the League of Nations and welcomed on her soil the United Nations headquarters as an appropriate symbol of the country's aspirations and as her indispensable instrument for world peace. In the postwar period the country produced her own Nobel Peace Prize winners in the persons of Ralph Bunche and Martin Luther King, Jr. The peace movement in the 1960s, moreover, was considerably stronger than the pacifism of the 1930s.

All of the above could represent real hope if the postwar years would not also have produced "the warfare state," to use the title of Fred J. Cook's recent book, a state with an ever-expanding military machine and an ever-growing military mind. At the end of his presidential career, in 1961, General Eisenhower delivered a farewell address that warned the American people of the growth of a "military-industrial complex" which was already exercising "unwarranted influence" over "every city, every state house, every office of the federal government."

Apparently the influence was already so firmly rooted that it remained unchecked and the colossus of military might and economic power kept right on growing. The Pentagon came to represent the mightiest concentration of military-economic power in the world, with over three million men under the latest arms, one-third of them deployed around the world to keep secure the economic empire, which in turn was expanding rapidly as a direct result of the arms industry. The concentration of military-economic power is paid for with a budget of over four times the spending of the world's largest corporation, General Motors; military land holdings exceed 27.6 million acres, larger than the state of Tennessee, including hundreds of bases overseas; military business occupies 22,000 prime contractors and 100,000 sub-contractors in 5,300 cities and towns; the military provides jobs for 10 percent of the labor force of 78 million, a conservative estimate.[10]

The military mind, Robert Leckie concludes, has become part of the American character:

> Where once we looked upon a large standing army as a threat to liberty, we now maintain a military force of more than three million young men, and to keep it supplied have levied against every American youth an eight-year "obligation" to service. To make certain that few youths escape the uniform, we have set up a vast reserve system and are reorganizing the National Guard. In the name of military security, or in the interests of success in the confrontation, we have given authority to the Federal Bureau of Investigation and a scope of operation to the Central Intelligence Agency to a degree that would have been unthinkable, let alone tolerated, three decades ago. Because of military security, a few of our fellow citizens, convened as the National Security Council, hold in their hands the life or death of us all. The activity of the executive branch—and sometimes even the legislative—is often hidden by a veil of secrecy as impenetrable as the Iron Curtain. Science serves military security; so does academia; giant industrial dynasties have been spawned by military needs, and the mammoth American economy—the envy and resentment of the world—is nourished in part by military or militarily-associated contracts.[11]

The official explanation for this development is that it began with the need to contain Communism in Europe and developed with the need to contain Communism in Asia. Be that as it may, it has now itself become an expensive and aggressive force that itself needs to be contained.

*　　*　　*

Economic policy and military program derive much of their strength from the prevailing religion, and therein we see a third major shift in America, from Sect-Christianity to State-Christianity.

The reference to Sect-Christianity is not in the traditional sense of narrowness or sectarianism, meaning smaller groups dissenting from an established church. Rather it points to the church as exercising separation from the state in a prophetic sense, a unique and creative witness that makes itself felt at home and abroad. The historic record of that witness in American life is sufficiently known that it need not be reported any further here.

State-Christianity, on the other hand, refers to a fusion of church and state to the point where a state religion emerges. To suggest that this may have happened in America is, I realize, to challenge popular history, which says that the very genius of America is the separation of church and state. After all, did not the founding fathers in adopting the First Amendment to the Constitution make a determined and dramatic break with church-state patterns of the past? And has that First Amendment not become almost as important to the American people as the First Commandment? And has the Supreme Court in recent years not produced a greater gulf of separation than ever?

The answer to all these questions may be affirmative, but separation in the prophetic sense has thereby not been established. The essence of separation does not lie in a constitutional provision nor in a given organizational pattern nor even in the interpretations of the highest court in the land. Nor is it to be found in geographic isolation or political noninvolvement.

The church loses its prophetic separateness when it becomes so identified with and immersed in the prevailing culture that it no longer represents its Lord and his word to that culture, when it accepts popular assumptions and nationalist values and all their cherished symbols. This does not happen by an overt change of theology. On the contrary, theology, doctrine, creeds, and vocabulary are often the last to be affected. The religious concepts, however, take new meanings. Discipleship begins to mean super-patriotism, the chosen people means Americans, the Kingdom of God means the kingdom of America, the banner of the cross really means the star-spangled banner, and dying for freedom translates itself into killing for freedom.

Even the person of Christ is made to take on the meaning of that culture. If the culture is racist, he is made over into the image of a racist. If the culture places a premium on capitalism and profiteering, then Christ becomes the champion capitalist. If the presidential leader has decided on a given war policy, even the preachers must not allow the word of God to challenge that policy. New meanings also make it entirely possible to relate the building of an economic empire and its protection by a military machine to the missionary task of the church. As one returned missionary from Vietnam said recently, "Everything I believe in and stand for is fought for right there in Vietnam." And then he asked for the bombing and annihilation of the Chinese enemy.[12]

To interpret State-Christianity in terms of Americanism is not to suggest that state religion is something new. On the contrary, it is as old as man, and in its most primitive forms is called tribal religion. Americanism is simply history repeating itself the nth time, and our surprise in discovering it here is only due to our foolish notion that the Constitution would prevent it and that Americans would never repeat the disastrous mistakes of older societies. Perhaps that is where the idolatry began, when they looked upon the Constitution as divine and America as infallible.

A nationalist religion, it should also be pointed out, is as much the product of the nation's leaders as it is the fault of a particular religion and its leaders. Tribal chieftains, caesars of all kinds, kings, queens, and presidents have usually wooed the dominant religion in order to strengthen corporate life. During World War II the Japanese emperor gained much of his strength from State-Shinto. It generated patriotism and turned all Japanese political aspirations and military crusades into the holy cause of State-Shinto.

And so it has been in "Christian" nations. The Russian czars found an alliance with the Orthodox church to be most convenient. The German princes in rebellion against Holy Roman power were delighted to find in Luther a champion of their cause. Winston Churchill was proud to have God on his side in his determination to destroy Germany. In twentieth-century Germanism, prior to 1945, we probably have the best European example of modern tribal religion or State-Christianity. And pan-Germanism was its internationalist missionary dimension. Wilhelm II said in 1914, as he sent his troops off to war: "Remember, the German people are the chosen of God. On me the German emperor, the spirit of God has descended. I am his sword, his weapon, his vice-regent."[13]

There we have a classic statement on nationalist religion. Substitute a few words in it like "world policeman" for "sword" and "America" for "German," and you have a fair summary of State-Christianity in America. But how, when, and where did Sect-Christianity become State-Christianity? To begin with an answer, we must remember that the Christian community in America was never completely one or the other. It was not always properly prophetic in the time of beginnings, nor has all the prophecy left it.

The religion of Americanism probably began with the Puritan Pilgrims. It was undoubtedly developed by their descendants. It was most certainly accelerated in the late nineteenth century when a mass campaign began to get new immigrants to accept the American customs, language, and way of life. From then on the American way of life became almost synonymous with the Jesus way of life, and the Americans became *This Almost Chosen People*, to use the title of Russel B. Neye's book.

The idea was strengthened by the world wars and songs like "God Bless America." It mushroomed during the imperial era after World War II, and most recently has been confirmed by such prominent national chaplains as Evangelist Billy Graham and the late Cardinal Spellman during and after Christmas tours of Vietnam. The ecumenical movement is probably as much a manifestation of Americanism as it is the discovery of a unity in Christ. Mass state education has also contributed its share. As Arnold Toynbee said:

> All the peoples in the world today are the devotees of the ancient and sinister worship of collective human power . . . the pagan religion of nation-worship. But children are indoctrinated in nation-worship in the United States more deliberately and more assiduously than any other country I have visited so far, except perhaps Argentina.[14]

In the fact of nation-worship, then, lies another cause of World War III. It turns humility into weakness and pride into virtue. It produces self-righteousness at the very moment when repentance is called for. It labels prophetic witness and action as treason. It turns unnecessary military adventures into holy crusades. It measures the costs of these crusades not in terms of humanity but in terms of American dollars and American lives. Nation-worship hardens hearts, closes minds, blocks the ears, and blinds the eyes to humanity and to the one and only living God. Nation-worship has always led to war and always will.

*   *   *

The blinding effect of a national idolatry or religion led to a fourth major shift in America, from an earlier passion for truth to an unprecedented participation in deception. Two of the most frequent themes in early American history are the exercise of freedom and the pursuit of truth. Both of these themes became one in the struggle of the press to be free from censorship and governmental control. The words of Milton's *Areopagitica* were spoken and written again and again to become part of the American outlook: "God himself is truth and the more honest anyone is in teaching truth to me, the more like God and the more acceptable to God he must be. It is blasphemous to believe that God is jealous of truth, that he does not wish it to spread freely among mankind."

Such a high respect for honesty and truth became the cornerstone of much of America's press system, her educational system, and her political system. Free and unhindered inquiry and expression were built into the Constitution and into the moral character of America. Although it was recognized that unrestricted inquiry and free expression would sometimes be painful it was believed in the long run always to be the most useful. Thus America built up a press, a university system, and a political pattern that became the envy of free men everywhere, as they recognized a degree of liberty rarely found elsewhere in such quantity and over such a long period of time.

As late as the end of 1967 the International Press Institute of Zurich praised official US news policy in Vietnam, saying that it "served as a useful example to those many governments who mistrust the press." That year, however, Malcolm W. Browne, a Pulitzer Prize reporter with a five-year tour in Vietnam, also told a magazine audience that all kinds of methods had been used to cover up the truth: direct lying, suppression of news, evasion of questions, the threat of withdrawing credentials from correspondents, and official whispering campaigns.[15] It was the year that William Tuohy of *The Los Angeles Times* reported that "any man who's ever been in the field . . . knows that there is no such thing as a body count. . . ."[16] It was the year that an aspirant for the American presidency, George Romney, told a Detroit television audience: "When I came back from Vietnam I had just had the greatest brain-washing that anybody can get when you go over . . . not only by the generals but also by the diplomatic corps over there, and they do a very thorough job. . . ."[17]

The problem of deception goes much deeper, however. It arises not only from the individual lies of officials but also from the total way American society sees itself and the world. Delusion and deception, in other words, are closely related to the religion of Americanism, which is incapable of truth at the highest levels, because it is itself untruth. Today we often wonder how nearly all of Germany could have had such a distorted view of reality as was common in the era of the Third Reich. The answer lies in Germanism. Once you have accepted the creed of "my country right or wrong," even the wrong becomes right. What serves the country by official or popular definition is right, whether it is right or wrong. In such a situation even truth-seeking journalists who want to be "patriotic," as well as professional, end up presenting the country in a rosy light when there is no justification for it.

Occasionally, of course, there are allusions to mistakes having been made, but the American pride will not allow their full admission or public confession. Pride, personal and national, demands that a story of failure somehow be turned into a success story. One gets the impression that American society would rather blow up the world than face the truth. And so, even though it knows the president is speaking an arrogant lie, it accepts his appraisal of the State of the Union, because untruth that feeds ego is somehow truth. No doubt this is why Mr. Johnson spoke as he did:

> If ever there was a people who sought more than mere abundance, it is our people. If ever there was a nation that was

capable of solving its problems, it is this nation. If ever there
was a time to know the pride and the excitement and the hope
of being an American it is this time.

But that is not the State of the Union. A more honest
message is the letter of a California family whose son died
in Vietnam and who knew what had really killed him:

> The selfish savagery of the society in which he lived; the
> inordinate pride and hypocrisy of the President, the compla-
> cent self-interest of the congressmen (whose sons don't go),
> the thirst of the military for power and prestige, and mad
> scramble of the war industries to grab and spend $75 billion
> this year, these are the things that destroyed our son, not the
> Viet Cong.[18]

* * *

Can we now understand what is happening, what is
turning the American way of life into the causes of World
War III? Economic greed and profiteering extending its
fingers into all parts of the world, depending on the
protection of a mighty military machine, both of which
are blessed and sanctified by the gods of a new American
religion, which through cunning and deception have suc-
ceeded in falsely posing as the one true God and falsely
presenting all their opponents as antichrists.

Admittedly, there are forces of change in American
society, as there were in Germany in the 1930s, seeking
movement in the opposite directions, namely from false-
hood and deception to honesty and truth, from state
religion to prophecy, from militarism to pacifism, and
from profiteering to proper sharing. But these forces are
few, and at the moment it appears that America, like
Germany, will not reverse her course until the shock treatment of going over the brink will wake her up.

NOTES TO ESSAY VII

1. Quoted in the *Ottawa Citizen*, August 9, 1967.
2. "Largest Peace-Time Armada," *The Canadian Mennonite*,
August 23, 1966, p. 1.

3. David Lawrence, "Vietnam—Our Great Philanthropy," *US News and World Report*, February 21, 1966, p. 112.

4. Dwight D. Eisenhower, *Mandate for Change* (New York: Doubleday, 1963), p. 333.

5. "Industry," *Time*, December 29, 1967, pp. 36ff.

6. *US News and World Report*, October 6, 1969, p. 62.

7. *US News and World Report*, November 13, 1967, p. 47.

8. Robert Leckie, *The Wars of America* (New York: Harper, 1968), pp. 13, 978.

9. J. A. Toews, "Significant Aspects of American Religious Pacifism in the Decade Prior to World War II," unpublished 1960 term paper, University of Minnesota.

10. Fred S. Hoffman, "The Pentagon Set-Up—World's Top Colossus," *Toronto Daily Star*, October 17, 1967, p. 1.

11. Leckie, *op. cit.*, pp. 978-979.

12. Quoted in the Toronto *Globe and Mail*, February 10, 1968, p. 4.

13. Wilhelm II in an address to his troops on August 4, 1914.

14. Arnold Toynbee, "Nation-worship as a Pagan Ritual," Toronto *Globe and Mail*, May 17, 1967, p. 7.

15. Malcolm W. Browne, "The New Face of Censorship," *True*, April 1967, pp. 39, 91-95.

16. Tom Wicker, "The Examiners of Vietnam," *New York Times*, January 14, 1968, p. E17.

17. WKBD-TV, Detroit, interview of Gov. Romney by Lou Gordon, reported in *Time*, September 15, 1967, p. 22.

18. "Selfish Pride Killed Our Son," quoted in the *Ottawa Citizen*, February 6, 1968, p. 6.

VIII

The Unrealism of Militarism

"All who take the sword die by the sword."
—Matthew 26:52

"The more I study the history of the world, the more I am convinced of the inability of brute force to create anything durable."
—Napoleon Bonaparte, after his exile to St. Helena

I propose in this essay to give a critique of militarism in our time from a pragmatic point of view. I do not intend to make a theological statement, and the reference to the New Testament above is not to be viewed as such. The quotation from Jesus, like the one from Napoleon, is a practical observation about life, a comment on human history that has proved true more often than not.

Not that Jesus (or for that matter Napoleon) was not also theological. On the contrary. The best insights from historical experience have often become the revelational content of theology. In much of the Bible history and theology are inseparable. We should not be surprised to discover today that the language of history, of practicality and realism, has much in common with theology, which has often been called the language of impractical idealism. Good theology is not impractical, and I intend to show that the burden of proof for realism rests not with the so-called idealists but with the militarists of this warring age.

Secondly, I do not intend to speak as a pacifist, certainly not in an absolute sense. One can—and all of us should—criticize the militarism of our age even if we were not baptized as pacifists. The alternatives we face are not necessarily limited to absolute pacifism and uncritical militarism.

In the third place, I shall not address all the standard questions thrown at those who criticize the military: Wouldn't you defend your wife and children if an armed attacker appeared at your door? Isn't social discipline necessary and desirable and isn't physical force an important ingredient in that discipline? Would you abolish the defense department completely and have a defense budget of zero? Would you disarm the police? All of these questions have their place and should not be avoided, but one need not be against a neighborhood police force to make the historical judgment that Nicholas of Russia had no business being the gendarme of Europe or Richard Nixon the policeman of the world.

Our question is a very practical one. At this point in history should the nations of the West, particularly of North America, continue in their defense policies, or should there be a retreat from the present escalating militarism?

The burgeoning militarism in both Canada and the United States is justified as a necessary and the only realistic response to the world situation today. Those who justify present policies and their escalation are for the most part quite sincere in believing that the threat and, if necessary, the use of military force on a greater or lesser scale will lead to the desired peace and world order. But are these assumptions correct? Is militarism really a realistic option for our society? If so, it seems to me, militarism must meet most or all of seven requirements examined in the remainder of this essay.

* * *

First, is militarism recommended by history? Man lives in large measure by his past experience, including his military experience. To be confident about his present militarism, he should have the strong encouragement of the historical record that this is the path to international peace. Can history give that recommendation?

It is true that one can extract from history the data one wishes to argue one's case just as a theologian can extract from the Bible the texts he needs to defend his point of view. So one can argue that peace comes as a result of war. One can point out that even the machinery of peace—the Congress of Vienna, the League of Nations, the United Nations—came as a result of major international conflagrations. This historical evidence might even lead us to conclude that true world federalism cannot come until the nations of this world have had another shock treatment or experienced the judgments of a World War III.

To argue that way, however, is simply to admit that dams and dikes have been built as a result of floods, that they have been built to prevent further floods, and that intelligent and watchful men could have and should have built them much sooner. It is also to say that wars are not the dikes themselves, as some would have us believe, but rather the floods.

The history of twentieth-century militarism is certainly a testimony to this. Two world wars, far from solving the world's problems, have compounded them almost infinitely. The seeds for most of the present international conflicts were sown by these two wars. The problems created and left by World War I became the causes of World War II. The Great War, fought to make the world safe for democracy, opened instead the floodgates to dictatorships of both the left and the right. Political and religious leaders have observed correctly that in many ways World War I turned out to be precisely the opposite of what it was thought to be.

World War I laid the foundations not only for further conflict in central Europe and for World War II but also for the present conflict in the Middle East. Even the War in Vietnam goes back to Versailles in 1919, when the victors refused to listen to Nationalist Ho Chi Minh, who wanted Indochina freed from French colonial subjugation.

World War II put down some dictators and empires, but it also restored the Russian empire and created the American empire, both of which together have since flouted more international law, exploited more peoples, and distributed more military stones instead of the bread of social and economic justice than any previous empires in all of history. And together now they are dangling the Damocles sword of a nuclear holocaust above the heads of three and a half billion people to protect their respective empires or, as they say, to promote peace and security.

Let the militarists demonstrate from history that rearmament does not lead to war, that military action has advanced the kingdom of truth, justice, love, and humanity more than destroyed it, and we will give them ear as having some practical solutions for our time. Until then we cannot look on them as very realistic.

*   *   *

A second question is whether the decisions of militarism are acceptable to humanity. The war game really works in a society only if that society has consented to the rules of the game. The age-old rule of the war game is that might makes right. Wars were fought on the mutual assumption that the victor made the decisions and the vanquished accepted them. The "unconditional surrender" policies of World War II, for instance, were still a product of the might-makes-right era.

Much has happened since 1945, however. There has been a great awakening of millions of formerly colonized peoples and a great stirring of the human conscience generally. The human race no longer accepts certain former standards of morality and legality. Humanity no longer recognizes poverty as inevitable nor racial subjugation as moral—witness the increasing isolation of South Africa in the world community.

Similarly, the human conscience has also been awakened on the war question, and the old rules are no longer acceptable, although the military brass around the world has not yet realized this. Even the military decisions of yesteryear are being reopened, as for example by the Indians and French of Canada. The Battle of the Plains of Abraham was not the British victory that our school books have suggested, we are now learning, two centuries later.

This is even more the case concerning contemporary military decisions. The Six-Day War of 1967 in the Middle

East was falsely so named. It was not finished in the six days, for the vanquished did not accept the military decision of the victor. As William T. Snyder has written:

> There is a parallel between Israel's experience with Arab resistance and the United States experience with Vietnamese resistance. In each case, it would be logical to come to terms with the stronger power but logic does not prevail when feelings run so deeply. I also believe that it is indicative of the dwindling power of the sword in present day world affairs.[1]

Perhaps nowhere has military impotence today been illustrated better than in Vietnam. By every equation of military mathematics, the Indochina War should have been won years before the inconclusive ceasefire of 1973. More firepower was applied there than in any previous conflict, and little Vietnam absorbed more bombs than all the world in World War II. Still the war did not end. At least one US general recommended bombing the Vietnamese "back into the Stone Age,"[2] but he did not explain how that would decide the issue, because by the emerging rules of the game that still would be no victory.

Some leaders, of course, still operate on the assumption that the big gun and the big threat is decisive, but every day proves them wrong. Every time, for instance, someone tells the separatists of Quebec, "You really cannot afford separatism," they reply, "If our enslavement by the economic powers-that-be is that great, separatism is the only thing we *can* really afford." Every time a Bruce Hutchison says that Canada dares not resist the Pentagon and pull out of NATO, because the Americans will knock the hell out of us if we do,[3] a Christopher Young, speaking for all self-respecting Canadians, responds: "If Hutchison is right, which I don't believe, his reports would lead . . . to the opposite conclusion: that we must break the bonds of this intolerable mercenary service at once."[4]

This breaking of the bonds of military oppression is becoming a universal mood. Confronted as they are by the diminishing power of the sword, the generals, instead of reversing their unrealistic policies, insist on bigger and sharper swords. As they do so, they are becoming the more unrealistic. In terms of its power over the human spirit, the sword is fast becoming an anachronism.

*　　*　　*

Third, we should ask whether the intelligence of militarism correctly identifies the true enemy. Admittedly, the military has a very sophisticated system for gathering so-called intelligence, and no one would dispute that a wealth of accurate data is at its disposal. But, after the Bay of Pigs or even the *Pueblo* incident, one would be a fool to place all one's confidence in military intelligence. Our question, however, does not mean to challenge the accuracy of the military's physical intelligence gathering. Much more critical are the attitudes and assumptions militarism brings to its electronic gear, which in my opinion are responsible for its continuing miscalculations of the world situation.

The military needs an enemy as much as the church needs a devil. Not only must this enemy be easily identified but the identification must be palatable to the people. Eastern militarists have found such an enemy in the so-called Imperialists; Western militarists in the so-called Communists. Both of them have had enough truth on their side to have allowed them to survive and thrive for nearly three decades. But both East and West have also been sufficiently in error so as to achieve major distortions in their intelligence and in the identification of the real enemies. The Soviet Union's real enemy in Czechoslovakia was not imperialism but nationalism, and France's and the USA's real enemy in Vietnam was not Communism but Vietnamese nationalism.

The militarists apparently never programmed the variable of nationalism into their computers. That is one reason why they did not always emerge with true intelligence. The Americans saw their main problem as located north of Saigon, when in fact it was in the delta to the south where millions of peasants, exploited for many years by their colonialist masters and absentee landowners, have long resisted the puppet administrators in Saigon.

This historical resistance to oppression seems also not to have been programmed into the computers, which is why

the military constantly miscalculated the degree of pacifi-
cation achieved in Vietnam by the military. As David
Halberstam says:

> The fact is that for 22 years the generals and their propa-
> gandists have been wrong, terribly wrong, about Indo-China,
> and they are wrong now. The enemy has total political superi-
> ority, his system works, and he can keep coming. . . .[5]

Unable to understand that the people were motivated
not by an imported Communism but by an ever-widening
and deepening nationalism, the militarists become blind
leaders. The tragedy was not so much that they were blind
but that they had also become the leaders in their society
at home, with the result that a whole enlightened people
was fooled.

> Many Americans will wonder how three administrations
> managed to delude themselves and the nation so convincingly
> and so long. For only stubborn self-delusion can explain our
> refusal to see the Vietnamese who fought hardest for national-
> ism and its living symbol Ho Chi Minh—not for the generals of
> Saigon; that patriotism more than Communism is what made
> them stand up to American might; and that our soldiers in
> Asia look no different to many of the longsuffering Viet-
> namese than the French who had been there earlier. Self-
> delusion has cost us dearly in blood, treasure, prestige, bitter
> dissent, strained alliances, and neglected priorities.[6]

As the military identifies as a monolithic Communism
national forces that are moving people all over the world,
it also overlooks other real causes of unrest in the world:
poverty, political oppression, and social and economic
injustice.

The military computers are not programmed to detect
the internal danger signals of social injustice, especially
when the military budget becomes a major factor in that
injustice. Gibbon and Toynbee have documented that civi-
lizations are more likely to be destroyed from within than
from without; still, military intelligence overlooks this and
other important variables.

To be critical of military intelligence is not to downplay
the value of burglar alarms or even of a system of detecting

enemy missiles in time for us to say our prayers. But if this is all we have, and if our system overlooks the bank robbing that goes on within, and if our radar does not measure the nationalistic winds that blow, our intelligence is inaccurate. If at a given point in history our high-priced intelligence misreads the world situation and does not detect the real enemy, how practical is it and how realistic is our militarism?

*   *   *

Fourth, does militarism provide security? There are two kinds of security to be considered here—psychological and physical. Of the two, psychological security is probably of foremost importance in a society that assumes the spirit of man to be of fundamental significance. Psychological security is not totally separable from physical security, of course. We feel more secure in a big city if we can lock our cars and hotel rooms, in a thunderstorm if we have shelter, and around strange dogs if they are on leashes.

Physical protection is, however, only part of the picture. A bigger factor is a person's spiritual serenity and mental equilibrium, which physical security cannot always provide and which can make a person secure even in the absence of physical props. Not infrequently these props even destroy psychological security.

The question we must face is whether the Western spirit has become more or less secure as it has surrounded its body with more and more defensive weaponry. The answer, I think, is obvious. Our heaping of weapons systems on weapons systems is indicative of the internal terror that remains. We sought security in a balance of power, which then became a balance of terror; and terror has become our chief problem.

We are not a secure society. We are like the multi-millionaire with an evil conscience, who, though he surrounds his house with high walls, hires his own security guards, rides in bullet-proof limousines, and stacks his money away in Swiss banks, is not really secure. His den is always shaking; his dogs are always barking; his dominoes are always falling.

We are a strange society. We claim the greatest God, the noblest constitutions, the best political system, the highest standard of living, the purest culture, the most just legal system, the largest military, and yet we are insecure. And the military cannot help us with this psychological problem. That being the case, it is unrealistic for the military to keep on claiming, and for us to keep on paying for, a psychological security that cannot be delivered.

Nor must we overlook the problems of physical security, for which high claims are also made. We can acknowledge the validity of some of the claims, for there has been no real mishandling of the powerful weapons. Hydrogen bombs accidentally lost off Spain and Iceland nonetheless remained safe. Yet those same military technologists who confidently claim no likelihood of accidents are also the ones who fear accidental Soviet launchings. At that point their own claims to technical infallibility become highly dubious.

There are other questions we must ask. At what point does a vast defensive military system become itself offensive and a major cause of insecurity? Is it not quite naive to suppose that the deployment of troops at hundreds of overseas bases, frequently against the will of local people, is purely defensive?

Moreover, is there anything in history to support our doctrine of deterrence? And if there is, has deterrence not been carried too far? Have any weapons of terror deterred any military establishments from producing even greater terror? And if they are not deterred from producing how will they be deterred from using? Does production not create its own momentum for action? And what about distribution? Is it not the height of unrealism to keep on heaping up arms around us while at the same time piling them up around the world at our own basis and in the hands of friendly military juntas, dictatorships, and other governments?

Our insecurity has not decreased but increased with the growth of our security system. To continue in our present policies is the height of unrealism.

*   *   *

A fifth point is that if militarism is to be a realistic option, it must not harm our value system or spirituality. Is this the case?

95

Military systems, budgets, and actions have always been justified as in the interests of values held to be dear. In the West we have said that our military activity is in the defense of freedom, of a value system and a way of life believed to be superior to all others.

To what extent are our assumptions correct? Is militarism really a defense of liberty or is it a threat to freedom? Robert Leckie has observed that only a few decades ago America believed freedom to be incompatible with a large standing army. No longer is this the case.[7]

Since the time of President Eisenhower's warning in 1961 that the size and power of the military-industrial complex was not a good omen for America, that complex has rapidly expanded.

Its influence has reached into every area of our continental life, so that universities, newspapers, politicians, and preachers have increasingly become a part of it. It has been responsible for the militarization of foreign policy and for allowing excessive military influence on our domestic life. A military coup has in some ways already been accomplished.

With this takeover has come not an increase but a decrease of freedom. In the foreign arena our militarism has meant alliances with dictators and military juntas who represent the very antithesis of freedom in Europe, Asia, and Latin America. In North America, militarism has contributed to the erosion of domestic freedom. Canada has lost more of its independence, and in the US the freedoms of its citizens have been increasingly subordinated to a misguided patriotism.

Truth has also suffered. In a military state truth must be subordinated to other purposes. The propaganda war, like the military war, chooses its means to serve its ends. The uses of propaganda and the failure of our "free" press to counteract it have destroyed truth in one way. The unwillingness of the military mind to repent and admit mistakes has destroyed it in another way. At the heart of the democratic system lies the continuous testing of truth and exposure of mistakes and weaknesses. Militarism cannot repent. It must keep on blundering in a desperate attempt "to save face" and "to end a situation with honor."

The real problem is mere human vanity. . . . It has been powerful men with vast egos, acting out the mistakes of the past as though it were mandatory to do so. Each time they came to the crossroads and were faced with a choice of plunging us further into something that was at best dubious, or admitting to a mistake, they plunged us further and further into it, putting their own feeling of infallibility above decency and common sense.[8]

We should, therefore, not be surprised that militarism cannot advance freedom and truth and our spirituality in general. Where civilization has not been able to overcome militarism, militarism has always destroyed civilization. Militarism is a law unto itself, which scorns the law of God and tramples human law under foot.

The question facing us is how long will we allow it to happen in our society. How long do we think we can be burdened down physically and preoccupied mentally with lethal weapons of every description and not suffer irreparable damage to our soul? How many lies can we tell, how many Asian whorehouses can we keep in business, how many unwanted red-haired babies can we leave behind in country after country, how many peasant families can we burn with napalm before we lose our self-respect? How many days, weeks, months, and years can a society hear reports of favorable kill ratios in Asia and not be thoroughly brutalized thereby? How much hell can we give to people before we get it ourselves?

Realism and practicality demand that, if the best in our value system is to be preserved, we must back away from our militarism.

* * *

In the sixth place, is militarism a positive contribution to a nation's social economy?

A common slogan during the Vietnam war was Lyndon Johnson's claim that the nation could afford both guns and butter. In a limited sense he was probably correct. In the same way that a bank can afford both, a burglar alarm system as well as a cafeteria, a nation can afford both. The one need not necessarily make impossible the other. Some economists have even argued that the military economy made possible the high standard of living and the high economic growth during the Johnson era. Indeed, it is commonly believed that the guns-economy has become so integrated with the butter-economy that the latter is dependent on the former and that it is impossible to separate the two.

It is easy to oversimplify the issues here and overlook important international and domestic considerations, both short-term and long-term. It has been acknowledged that Vietnam created a payments-deficit problem for the US, but it has not been recognized that this problem would have been completely unbearable for the economy if the arms trade on the one hand and the use of cheap labor in foreign investments on the other would not have offset the Vietnam losses.

The international arms trade and arms race raises the guns-and-butter question on a worldwide basis. Total arms spending each year is now in excess of $160 billion—at a time when the world's masses are in desperate need of educational, medical, agricultural, and other economic assistance. The implications of this unrealistic approach to the human situation are clear in growing unrest and violent revolution. We are beginning to see before our very eyes that the world cannot afford both guns and butter.

The same observation can be made in the USA. The monetary and human resources so badly needed for the renewal of the urban environment and for minimal socio-economic justice for the exploited and oppressed are poured into new weapons projects. In his first inaugural address, Mr. Nixon spoke of lifting up the poor and hungry. How is this to be done if the nation does not shift its priorities and cause militarism to take a back seat?

The chief threats to global security are not those of external armies or weapons but the seething unrest of masses of unhappy people suffering from economic want and social injustice. Before our very eyes it is becoming true that no society can afford both guns and butter to the extent that it is now being attempted. It is unrealistic, therefore, to continue to allow military spending to dominate the social economy of our society. And we have not even begun to consider the socio-economic deficit brought about by the waste of human and material resources in current military programs.

*　　*　　*

In the light of all the foregoing, if militarism is to be a realistic option for our society it must be the only available strategy. Is it?

"What do we do if we don't bomb?" The words of a military officer in Saigon in 1966 keep ringing in my ears. They are symbolic of the one-track mind of the military. Its strategies of response to domestic or international conflict are limited to the use of military force.

This inability even to recognize alternate strategies was so clearly evident in the Western military response to the 1968 Soviet intervention in Czechoslovakia. At the very time the Czechs were testing a nonconventional strategy of confronting military force, our militarists had not a creative contribution to make. All they could think of was more of the same thing.

The militarists, of course, are not to be blamed alone, for society has not demanded anything better. Efforts for disarmament have been weak. There has been very little clamor for peace chairs and peace research at our universities. Nor have churches been particularly courageous and creative in seeking and espousing nonviolent strategies for conflict resolution.

Yet, enough has already been said, done, and written in the area of nonviolent strategies to commend the possibilities to universities for teaching and research, to politicians for policy considerations, and to defense departments for experimentation and testing.

The Czech model of resistance, for instance, could for Canada become the only practical and realistic defense. Or in what way will we defend ourselves against any military threats or oppression from any of the super-powers? For Canada to consider traditional defense systems against either the USSR or the USA is totally unfeasible.

In a sense, our political leaders have already recognized the need for nonviolent strategies to achieve political ends. The fanatical separatists of Quebec and the militant leaders of the ghetto revolts are told that violence is not the way. But if bombs and guns are not the way for them as "sovereign" individuals why should violence still be the way for "sovereign" nations?

In the arena of domestic conflict, the late Martin Luther King, Jr., inspired by Gandhi and Jesus of Nazareth, developed nonviolent strategies of considerable impact. These were by no means perfected or totally effective, but it would be difficult for any single man to equal his contribution to the nonviolent resolution of conflict and the achievement of social justice.

There are other historical models, focused in persons, movements, or events, that can give us guidance for our time. Consider Jewish nonviolence and Roman military power under Caligula in the first century; or the pacifism of colonial Pennsylvania; or the six-month Arab strike against the policies of the Mandatory Palestine Government in the 1930s; or Norwegian nonviolent resistance against the Nazis in the 1940s; or Russian resistance in the Vorkuta concentration camp in 1953.[9]

In 1966 Lyndon Johnson pledged the US to an assistance program amounting to one billion dollars to harness and develop the water resources of the Mekong River, which begins in China and flows through Laos, Thailand, Cambodia, and Vietnam. It seemed to be a very generous offer, but in the light of the billions expended since then in military activity, it was a pittance.

What might Vietnam be like now if all the thousands of Americans who went to Vietnam had left uniforms and guns at home and instead gone with overalls and spades to work on that Mekong project under UN auspices. Not much imagination or prophetic insight is required to conclude that in all probability:

—far fewer Americans and Vietnamese would be dead today;

—the Southeast Asian economy would be in better shape;

—the political situation would be sounder and stabler;

—Chinese and Russian influence would be weaker;

—American prestige all over the world would be higher.

It is clear that, in Vietnam at least, almost any other strategy than the military one would have been better. And so it has been and will be also in other conflict situations.

It is only proper to admit that on some of our questions the evidence is ambivalent. One can argue for and against militarism in the same way that one can argue from the available data that crime does not pay and that it does pay.

But we have heard the pro-militarism arguments so often that we have been propagandized into thinking that that's the way it is. As we have examined these arguments we have discovered, however, that they do not stand up and that there is another side to the story.

That side of the story, for all the reasons stated above, needs now to be proclaimed from the rooftops. Militarism has failed our society by claiming and asking too much for itself while giving humanity such a questionable return. It is time to call a halt. It is time to proclaim judgment and to invite repentance. It is time to insist not only on a review but on a reversal of our policies.

The case for reducing our military establishments and the budgets is so strong—if we do not, they will be the cause of our destruction—that statesmen (and even politicians) should not feel any dilemmas in their decision-making. And pacifistic theologians can step forth boldly as the champions of a very practical idealism. The burden of proof for realism rests with the military.

NOTES TO ESSAY VIII

1. Wm. T. Snyder, "The Six-Day War Goes On," *MCC News Service*, March 7, 1969, p. 5.

2. General Curtis E. LeMay, quoted by the Toronto *Globe and Mail*, October 4, 1968, p. 8.

3. Bruce Hutchison, "What a Split from NATO Could Cost Canada," in the Toronto *Globe and Mail*, February 21, 1969, p. 7.

4. Christopher Young, "The Big Threat," *Ottawa Citizen*, March 1, 1969, p. 6.

5. David Halberstam, "President Nixon and Vietnam," *Harpers Magazine*, January 1969, p. 24.

6. Editorial in *Look*, January 21, 1969, p. 19.

7. Robert Leckie, *The Wars of America* (New York: Harper, 1968), pp. 978-979.

8. Halberstam, *op. cit.*

9. For readings on these and other examples see Mulford Q. Sibley, *The Quiet Battle* (New York: Doubleday, 1963).

IX

The Unilateral Disarmament of the Church

> *"They shall beat their swords into mattocks and their spears into pruning knives; nation shall not lift sword against nation nor ever again be trained for war."* —Isaiah 2:4

God's goal for humanity is a world without war, without the instruments of war, and without the mentality of war. He has registered this goal as an eternal hope within the human breast and as a recurrent theme in the literature of the human race. One of the most stirring of such passages in the Hebrew-Christian writings is the vision of a universal reign of peace and justice spoken by Isaiah, son of Amoz, quoted above.

This projection of the nations of the world subjecting their nationalist ambitions to the will of the sovereign God and governing by his light has its parallels in the New Testament literature, notably in the Revelation to John. In his vision (Revelation 21, 22) John saw the national societies surrendering their pride and their glory and finding true healing and freedom in subordination to the throne of God.

Extrascriptural examples of this vision are too numerous to mention, since they can be found both among primitive peoples and more sophisticated societies. Henry Wadsworth Longfellow, for instance, records the following Indian version of Isaiah's dream in *The Song of Hiawatha:*

Buried was the bloody hatchet;
Buried was the dreadful war-club;
Buried were all war-like weapons,
And the war-cry was forgotten.
There was peace among the nations.

Among the more modern countries of Europe in the seventeenth, eighteenth, and nineteenth centuries an impressive number of individuals and societies brought forth internationalist peace proposals to rid Europe of the scourge of war. Most of their ideas were related to Isaiah and John, who, as we have already seen, saw the nations linked together by a common bond, the gospel being the supreme law, and mediation being substituted for war. Men like William Penn, John Bellers, the Abbé Saint-Pierre, Jeremy Bentham, Immanuel Kant, and Leo Tolstoy concerned themselves with plans for international organization.[1]

* * *

The problem of the twentieth century, however, is that we have perfected the weapons of war, multiplied their use in global conflict, and found no way of disengaging ourselves in spite of the assistance of such instruments as the United Nations. Indeed, we find ourselves confronted worldwide with growing expenditures for defense systems, with the USA spending nearly half that amount. At the heart of the arsenal are the nuclear weapons, of which a special UN Task Force of Nuclear Arms Escalation reported the following:

> There is one inescapable and basic fact. It is that the nuclear armories which are in being already contain large megaton weapons, every one of which has a destructive power greater than that of all the conventional explosive that has ever been used in warfare since the day gunpowder was discovered. Were such weapons ever to be used in numbers, hundreds of millions of people might be killed, and civilization as we know it, as well as organized community life, would inevitably come to an end in the countries involved in the conflict. Many of those who survived the immediate destruction . . . would suffer from long-term effects of irradiation and transmit to their offspring a genetic burden which would become manifest in the disabilities of later generations.[2]

Every effort to halt the armaments race and to bring about even modest disarmament on a lasting basis has failed. It is true that there were temporary disarmaments. Germany was disarmed after World War I. In 1921-22 France, Italy, Japan, Great Britain, and the United States agreed to limit the number, size, and guns of their battleships for fifteen years. In 1930 Japan, Great Britain, and the United States consented to limit the size and guns of their cruisers, destroyers, and submarines. But it is also true that Germany began to rearm in 1933 and that other agreements lasted only until 1936, as all efforts of the League of Nations disarmament conferences failed. The consequences are familiar to all.

The peace treaties of World War II again provided for the disarmament of certain nations, but general disarmament became even more problematic than after World War I. The United Nations General Assembly set up a twelve-nation Disarmament Commission in 1952, enlarging it to twenty-six members in 1957 and to the full UN membership in 1959. The membership expansion brought the advantage of universal involvement and the disadvantages of limited efficiency and achievement.

Since the early 1960s smaller international groups, such as the eighteen-nation committee created in 1962, have been meeting periodically to work on the problem, and some nations have created their own task forces, such as the United States Arms Control and Disarmament Agency set up in 1961. But all disarmament efforts have made little progress, mainly for the reason that Canadian Prime Minister Lester B. Pearson cited when he accepted the Nobel Peace Prize: "we prepare for war like precocious giants, for peace like retarded pygmies. . . . "[3]

Yet, the nations could not relax their efforts entirely. Frightened by the monster they were creating and prodded by leading scientists of the Pugwash Movement and by a 1958 petition with the signatures of 11,000 scientists from forty countries they kept on working, and with some results. In 1963 the USA and the USSR signed the Nuclear Test Ban Treaty prohibiting nuclear weapons tests in the atmosphere, in outer space, and underwater. In 1966 the United Nations General Assembly adopted a treaty on principles governing the activities of states in the exploration and use of outer space and specifically banning the orbiting of "any objects carrying nuclear weapons or any other kinds of weapons of mass destruction." This "demilitarization of outer space treaty" was signed simultaneously in London, Moscow, and Washington in January 1967.

The USA and USSR recently agreed on a nonproliferation treaty, which is seen by them as a significant arms control measure. Since the treaty, however, does not provide for nuclear stockpile reduction by the super-powers, it is seen by other powers as an attempt to deny them what the USA and USSR are not really willing to give up themselves. Hence, it is difficult for the world community to accept the treaty. So the arms race continues with no end in sight.

*   *   *

Since multilateral and bilateral disarmament appear to be out for reasons of international politics and national pride, some pacifist spokesmen have suggested that disarmament should be unilateral, by whichever nation has the wisdom and courage to accept the challenge. That, too, appears to be an unlikely possibility. The proposal is viewed as impractical, though it must still be demonstrated that multilateral rearmament is more practical. The UN Task Force at least has come to the conclusion that the nuclear arms escalation is only increasing insecurity and unendingly complicating the problems it was meant to solve.

In spite of its unpopularity, "impracticality," and "impossibility," as the politicians would say, unilateralism appears to be the call of the hour. If humanity cannot collectively do what is necessary to prevent the ultimate in the destruction of God's creation, individuals or groups of individuals must move out alone to represent in word and in deed the vision of a disarmed world. And preposterous as the suggestion may seem to the worldly wise, such an approach is not really that far out. Common sense alone suggests that outright rejection of the present military madness could be quite reasonable.

Besides, the history of mankind supports this approach. Much progress has come by way of unilateralism. The

105

human race moves ahead when individuals or groups carry forward with determination and perseverance an idea or a cause that does not have wide popular support. The present causes of majorities were always first the causes of minorities.

Unilateralism also finds its support in Christian theology. Again and again, God and his prophets have acted unilaterally to save the people. Again and again the people have rejected the prophets. But this has not prevented God from acting again. He sent his Son, in the supreme act of unilateral love. Similarly, the Son's obedient coming was a unilateral act of faithfulness to the will of the Father. Seen by the worldly wise, Jesus was a fool whose views and manner of life took him to the cross. Today we acknowledge that it was precisely the unilateral risk he took and sacrifice he made which contributed to the salvation of the world.

Jesus was followed in his approach by a small band of disciples whom he had recruited and instructed, and by the church, which they founded. It was only a small flock, a minority movement, but because of its faithfulness to the kingdom idea, it was nevertheless " . . . a chosen race, a royal priesthood, a dedicated nation, and a people claimed by God for his own" (I Peter 2:9).

The church was always meant to be God's avant-garde, the innovator of his kingdom, the pioneer of the new order. Though the church failed its Lord many times, at its best it could never accept sin, disease, illiteracy, poverty, slavery, injustice, and inequality. At its best it could never accept war. Countless times its members followed Jesus into persecution and martyrdom rather than give up an idea. Its first concern was not that which appeared to be effective, that which was politically expedient, that which brought economic security, but rather that which represented the kingdom. At its best, the church has always seen a unilateral expression on earth of the will of God as it was in heaven.

This is the church's calling also today. As the carrier of Isaiah's vision, as an extension of the body of Christ, and as an international community, the church, more than any other agency, is in position to give to the world the unilateral witness that is needed. Ideally the church is free from all those things which prevent disarmament: the need to satisfy national pride, the need to be economically secure, the need to survive physically. The church does not have to be secure or survive. It is free to do God's bidding. Moreover, the church's specialty is to bring about change, first where it matters most in the inner man. As the military machine arises from a military mind so disarmament issues from the disarmed heart.

What is true in theory is not always true in practice. The church has often lost its vision as it became involved with the ambitions of this world and the struggle for security. Following an early emphasis on pacifism, the Christian church learned to accept the theory of the just war, to bless the Crusades, to promote the wars of religion, and finally to undergird the wars of the respective nation-states.[4]

Today the warlike stance of the Christian community is attested to in a number of ways. The Canadian Peace Research Institute discovered "that Christians are more war-like in their attitudes than non-Christians."[5] C. Wright Mills observes that religion has become a subordinate part of the overdeveloped national society:

> If there is one safe prediction about religion in this society, it would seem to be that if tomorrow official spokesmen were to proclaim XYZ-ism, next week 90 percent of religious declaration would be XYZ-ist. At least in their conforming rhetoric, religious spokesmen would reveal that the new doctrine did not violate those of the church. As a social and as a personal force, religion has become a dependent variable. It does not originate; it reacts. It does not denounce; it adapts. It does not set forth new models of conduct and sensibility; it imitates. . . . The verbal Christian belief in the sanctity of human life has not of course been affected by the impersonal barbarism of twentieth century war. But this belief does not itself enter decisively into the plans now being readied for World War III. A savage politician once asked how many divisions the Pope had—and it was a relevant question. No one need ask how many chaplains any army that wants them has. The answer is: as many as the generals and their other satraps feel the need of. Religion has become a willing spiritual means and a psychiatric aide of the nation-state.[6]

The armament race presents an opportunity for the

church, but the worldwide mood for disarmament and against war doubles that opportunity. The vocal supporters of disarmament include leading teachers, clergymen, women, students, lawyers, economists, architects, engineers, planners, businessmen, artists, writers, actors, and social workers. A favorable national and international climate for a brave unilateral witness exists. How can the church—or even a minority within it—rise to the occasion and seize the opportunity of the hour.

As one surveys the weaknesses of the church, it appears that God's minority movement would be strengthened if it could experience a thoroughgoing psychological and economic liberation, on the one hand, and a theological and political reorientation, on the other hand.

Like the rest of our society, the church is beset by fear. Government-sponsored surveys show that 82% of Americans sleep behind locked doors and 37% have guns in their homes for protection. And many leaders call for more police and guns even for the domestic situation. That a man who has no God and no sense of immortality should feel insecure is clear to us, but we are a society whose testimony is "In God We Trust."

Albert Camus has called "the seventeenth century . . . the century of mathematics, the eighteenth century that of the physical sciences, and the nineteenth century that of biology; our twentieth century is the century of fear."[7] Admitting that to be so, most of us will be inclined to find the cause of our fears outside of ourselves. And well there may be objective reasons for our fear, but the main reasons are subjective. Our fears arise not from the external enemy being so great as that our internal resources are so small. Fear fills the vacuums in our life created by the loss of faith, by the fading of love, the extinction of hope, the retreat of knowledge, and the absence of humility. Fear accompanies doubt, hate, hopelessness, ignorance, pride, and dishonesty. Our fears are the fears of a rich man who has more than his share of the world's wealth, the fears of the guilty running away from the law and from God, the fears of the selfish unwilling to share when conscience tells them they must. Much of the fear we blame on Communists actually originates with our consciences.

It is urgent for the times in which we live that at least

believers be liberated from their fears. The man filled with fear soon becomes a terror for others. The man without fear is the truly disarmed man. Jesus spent considerable time teaching his disciples that the man of faith should be free from fear. He should not fear a hostile environment and not a hostile humanity. He should not even fear persecution and death.

It goes without saying that a faith even as small as a grain of mustard seed could give us more security than the mountains of weapons we have stock-piled. Disarmament begins with a liberation from our fears, and a witness against armament can only proceed from people who have been saved from fear. God wants to save us now and make us so courageous that we can go through the fire for him.

I have a suspicion that much of the American fear is the fear of the rich man tied to his wealth. Liberation from fear, therefore, really means liberation from property. Both are absolute prerequisites for unilateral disarmament. To be freed from fear and from property is to be freed from dependence on the military. To be freed from such dependence is to have been internally, unilaterally disarmed.

Our liberation from property could begin with a new concept of it. This is one area in which God's new morality has made little difference on the old morality of man's tradition and jungle law. In many other areas we have assumed that the law of the land is not necessarily the law of God, but not with respect to property. Our present law has two dimensions: one primitive and the other quite sophisticated. The primitive part says that if you seize a given property and hold it by force it is yours. The more sophisticated part says that if you can secure legal title to a property by paying for it what is required and agreed upon, it is also your own.

Both of these concepts of property are devoid of any high morality. There is no hint of stewardship in them. Yet the law of God relates all property to stewardship, because "the earth is the Lord's and all that is in it, the world and those who dwell therein . . . " (Psalm 24:1), which is another way of saying that the world and all its resources belong to all of humanity. If a man is set over a property, he is, by the law of God, set over it as a steward. In the eyes of

God, the property is man's only as long as he does not exploit it and horde it at the expense of the rest of humanity, present and future. Even the children of Israel, who were told that Canaan was being given to them "forever," were told that "forever" ended with disobedience. Possession was tied to covenant and covenant implied stewardship. Israel as a steward had a responsibility both toward the land and toward the neighbors. Perpetual ownership was guarded against by the law of redistribution, which was applied every fifty years.

Measured by this higher law of property we of the West stand condemned. Our polluted soil, water, and air attest to the fact that we are robbing our children. The familiar commentary that "the rich get richer . . . and the poor get poorer" is witness to the fact that we are robbing our world neighbors. Our expenditures for defense are witness to the fact that we are robbing everybody. All our transactions may be legal, and by that standard lawful, but they could by another standard be grossly immoral. In the law courts of God, the biggest thieves may not be the poor who seize what is not their own by means of riots and revolution but the rich who have kept what is not their own by craftiness and the protection of the courts. In God's sight we have lost title the moment we have taken for ourselves more than our share. And this taking has happened in many ways: by immoral investment, by selfish protectionism, by ruthless military action and by inadequate giving.

Our acceptance of a new concept of property will already be the beginning of the needed theological reorientation. There are probably a number of areas in which rethinking and reformulation are necessary, but crucial to our present problem is the idea of the kingdom of God as our goal on the one hand, and the cross as a method of achieving it on the other.

Again we must come back to the visions of Isaiah and John, and to the clear implications of Jesus' role as a king and of his prayer "Thy kingdom come; thy will be done on earth as it is in heaven." All of these remind us of the goal, which is for the "sovereignty of the world [to pass] to our Lord and his Christ" (Revelation 11:15).

This means that the kingdom really embraces the whole

world and all its little kingdoms, be they personal, social, commercial, or political. All must be brought under the Lordship of Christ, who for that reason is called King of kings. The wise men from the east recognized him as a King; Herod feared him as a King; the authorities crucified him as a King; and his followers crowned him as a King.

Thus to acknowledge Christ and his kingdom is not to have achieved its complete victory, but it means to have made a beginning. Once the kingdom of God is within us it can become something outside of us. Once it is within us, we have given it a beginning, and we can pray for its coming and its appearance in fulness.

The manner of its coming arises in part from the inevitable opposition to the King and his kingdom. The kings of this world do not surrender their kingdoms and their sovereignties without a fight. The promoters of Christ's kingdom therefore are under temptation likewise to fight to gain ground for him. They are, to draw an analogy from the Reformation, always in danger of becoming Muensterites.[8] The disciples were tempted. Unable to convert a Samaritan village, they asked Jesus for permission to call in "fire from heaven" (Luke 9:51-56). Jesus rebuked them. Peter cut off Malchus' ear, but Jesus said that the sword was no way to bring in the kingdom. He himself was tempted to call in legions, but he knew that that would be forfeiting rather than advancing the cause (Matthew 12:47-56).

In word and deed, in life and in death, Jesus taught that the way to bring in the kingdom was by way of the cross. To him the cross was a way *of* life as well as a gate *to* the crown of the kingdom. The cross is both an involuntary suffering resulting from the resistance of the world's kingdoms, and a voluntary experience of suffering. Voluntarily, unilaterally, the disciple disarms by accepting the cross. He denies his rights for others. He accepts injustice so that the cause of justice may be advanced. He faces persecution if this is necessary for truth to have its witness. He allows himself to be killed so that the vicious cycle of war is broken. He accepts crucifixion, because it is better that the innocent die for the sins of the people, than that the innocent destroy the people.

This new way of looking at the kingdom and the cross

inevitably brings about a new way of looking at the empire and at the gun. In other words, a theological reorientation brings about a political sensitization. The life of a disciple leads to the role of a prophet.

Suddenly the assumption that our government is on God's side and that God is on our government's side becomes questionable. Suddenly we discover the extent to which the American way of life has strayed away from the kingdom and the extent to which American sovereignty has challenged the sovereignty of Christ. Suddenly, we wake up to the fact that government is against God when it insists on national sovereignty, on economic protectionism, when it misuses its vast resources, depends for physical and spiritual security on military power, when it enters into unholy alliances, when it mistreats its own and other peoples, and when it tells lies to hide its evil deeds.

* * *

But what shape does this witness take? What are some of its consequences? To begin with, we might say that the liberated and reorientated Christian presence is already a part of the witness. To be free from fear and free from property *is* to be a light in society. To have taken up the cross in pursuit of the kingdom *is* to be salt. A significant witness is therefore inherent in unilateral disarmament. The disarmed Christian has an effect on the American empire in the same way that pacifist Christianity had effect on the Roman empire:

> The introduction of Christianity had some influence on the decline and fall of the Roman empire . . . the last remnants of the military spirit was buried in the cloisters; a large portion of public and private wealth was consecrated to . . . charity and devotion. . . .[9]

More needs to be said about the particular forms of the contemporary witness. One of its dimensions is certainly resistance to nation-worship. Nation-worship is as real a temptation for us as for the Christians of the Roman empire and the German Christians during the era of the Third Reich. To give Americanism a Christian halo does not change the fact. A nation is known more by the fruits of its imperialism than by its pious propagandistic claims.

In such a context, the Christian witness has political relevance and content. The followers of the King of kings can no more escape political implications than he could, offending as he was to both the Jews and the Romans. Nor can they escape it anymore than Paul could escape it as a preacher of the gospel and as a martyr in Rome. His preaching in Thessalonica had already produced the accusation that he was flouting the decrees of Caesar, saying that there was another king, Jesus (Acts 17:6-9).

The witness on behalf of the great white throne and him who sits on it must also have some relevance to the White House and him who sits in it. There is a widespread notion that the separation of church and state prevents the church from proclaiming the King and his kingdom to government officials. But what of Nathan's rebuke of King David (II Samuel 12:7)? Or the witness of Elijah and Micaiah before King Ahab (I Kings 21:20)? And Daniel's witness before King Belshazzar (Daniel 5:22)? Or John the Baptist before Herod (Matthew 14:4)? And Jesus identifying himself as King before Pilate (Matthew 27:11)? Should Dietrich Bonhoeffer really not have offended his Fuehrer? What about the Baptist preachers in the Soviet Union and the faithful Reformed in South Africa? And how about the Anabaptist Reformer, Menno Simons, whose zeal was always in bad taste and whose sharp tongue always appeared to be rude, to wit?

> When I think to find a magistrate who fears God, who performs his office correctly and uses his sword properly, then verily I find as a general rule nothing but a Lucifer, an Antiochus, or a Nero, for they place themselves in Christ's stead so that their edicts must be respected above the word of God. Whosoever does not regulate himself according to them and does not serve Baal, but maintains the ceremonies of Christ and lives according to the Word of God, such a one is arrested as a hoodlum and made to suffer his property confiscated. . . . Besides we have their unreasonable pomp, pride, greed, uncleanness, lying, robbing, stealing, burning, hatred, envy, avarice, and idolatry. Yet they want to be called Christian princes and gracious lords. O Lord! . . . [10]

Closely related to the witness in high places and low is the complete dissociation from the military establishment.

This can mean many things. It certainly should mean personal conscientious objection.

Christians are normally most anxious to obey the authorities, but they cannot in good conscience do so when the authorities themselves are disobeying God. Almost every major Christian theologian (Tertullian, Origen, Augustine, Wycliffe, Luther, Calvin, and Aquinas) has held that under certain circumstances it is right for Christians to resist the civil authorities, believing like Peter that we must obey God rather than man (Acts 5:29).

Dissociation should also mean nondependence on the military for protection, particularly if this means the execution of any number of other people, and also the refusal to accept a military crusade on the grounds that it represents protection and extension of the gospel. Is there not something very terrible about Western troops rescuing Western missionaries in the Congo by shooting hundreds of blacks? Has the time not come for Christians to insist that in their service abroad their lives are no more precious than the lives of the people they have come to serve, not in need of any greater security and protection, and not always in need of evacuation every time the red alert goes on? As Menno Simons said:

> Our weapons are not weapons with which cities and countries may be destroyed, walls and gates broken down, and human blood shed in torrents like water. But they are weapons with which the spiritual kingdom of the devil is destroyed and the wicked principle in man's soul is broken down: We have and know no other weapons, besides this, the Lord knows, even if we should be torn into a thousand pieces, and if as many false witnesses rose up against us as there are spears in the fields, and grains of sand upon the seashore.[11]

The consequences of the bold proclamation and the radical witness, of course, are clear. Those who unreservedly and unilaterally disarm and commit themselves to the vision of Isaiah and the kingdom of our Lord must expect insult, outrage, suffering, and harassment. Society will forsake them. Some popular preachers will denounce them. The FBI will watch them. The military will pursue them. And the courts will jail them.

As the crisis deepens some may even be charged with

treason and put to death. Yet, as those who were persecuted before them, they will have the satisfaction and the
joy of giving continuity to Isaiah's vision, of contributing
to a warless world, of bringing in the kingdom. By faith
they know that posterity will call them blessed and that
they will hear the Lord saying, "Well done, good and
faithful servant" (Matthew 25:21, 50).

NOTES TO ESSAY IX

1. See Peter Mayer, *The Pacifist Conscience: Classic Writings on
Alternatives to Violent Conflict from Ancient Times to the Present*
(New York: Holt, Rinehart, and Winston, 1966), pp. 66-67.

2. "The Nuclear Time Bomb: Report to UN Secretary General U
Thant by the Task Force on Nuclear Arms Escalation," *Saturday
Review*, December 9, 1967, pp. 16-17, 70-75.

3. Lester B. Pearson, "The Four Faces of Peace," Nobel Peace
Prize Acceptance Speech, 1957.

4. Roland H. Bainton, *Christian Attitudes Toward War and Peace*
(Nashville: Abingdon, 1960).

5. Norman Z. Alcock, "What We've Learned Through Peace Research," *The Observer*, December 15, 1965, pp. 18-19, 40.

6. C. Wright Mills, "A Pagan Sermon to the Christian Clergy,"
The Nation, March 8, 1958.

7. Albert Camus, "Neither Victims nor Executioners," *Politics*,
July-August 1947.

8. C. J. Dyck, *Introduction to Mennonite History* (Scottdale: Herald, 1967), pp. 77-78.

9. Edward Gibbon, *Decline and Fall of the Roman Empire.*

10. Menno Simons, "Not Cease Teaching and Writing," *The Complete Writings of Menno Simons*, pp. 298-299.

11. Menno Simons, "Foundation of Christian Doctrine," *ibid.*, p.
198.

X

The Church and Nationalism

> *Jesus said, "Pay Caesar what is due to Caesar, and pay God what is due to God."* —Mark 12:17

> *Peter and John said to them in reply: "Is it right in God's eyes for us to obey you rather than God?"* —Acts 4:19

> *Every person must submit to the supreme authorities. There is no authority but by act of God, and the existing authorities are instituted by him.* —Romans 13:1

> *I urge that petitions, prayers, intercessions, and thanksgivings be offered for all men; for sovereigns and all in high office.* —I Timothy 2:1

> *Submit yourself to every human institution for the sake of the Lord, whether to the sovereign as supreme or to the governor as his deputy.* —I Peter 2:13-14

Those words from the sacred writings are the ones quoted most often in our churches as we examined our Christian obligations to the state. Our usual interpretation of their collective meaning called for obedience to the state except when the demands of the state and of our national cultures were in conflict with what we believed to be the will of God.

Today there appears to be considerable uncertainty about the church's relation to the state. We must take a critical look at ourselves and at our nationalism so that we may rediscover the stance that God wants us to take. It seems to me we can do this best by asking a series of questions concerning the meaning and nature of the various nationalisms that confront us.

* * *

First, does nationalism mean maturation or retardation for our society? As we look into the history of man, we observe that nations came about when a number of tribes in a geographical area or a number of provinces or states agreed that it was best for them to cooperate rather than compete with each other. They formed nation-states, which made cooperation possible. In that sense, nationalism was a positive development because it allowed for the rearrangement of society for its total good.

It is also true, however, that nation-states themselves became tribal in their orientation, with the result that they ended up warring among themselves. The wars of the twentieth century are perfect examples of the tribal problem of nationalism.

Nationalism needs to give way to a higher stage of human organization in the same way that tribal organization needed to give way to something higher. The European Common Market or the United States of Europe may provide such an answer for Europe.

Observing the total international picture today, we can see some nation-states that are quite young. For these nationalism is a step of maturation, away from tribal organization or from colonial dependence. Other nationalisms, however, are older, and to the extent that they insist on their nationalism as the ultimate end of their national development, nationalism represents retardation.

Nationalism in the development of a nation can be compared to adolescence in the experience of an individual. It is a necessary stage of development, but it should be only temporary. After infancy, adolescence is a sign of maturation. As a permanent stage preventing adult maturity, it represents retardation.

A second, related question asks whether we are talking about nationalism or about imperialism. Older nation-states, which have become strong powers, often fail to realize the extent to which their maturity and strength has become a factor of domination in other societies. This was surely true of the Czarist Russian empire and of the British empire. The French and the Portuguese also have had great difficulty in recognizing the extent to which the extension of their nation became a problem to their colonial dependencies. France had to learn from a very bitter experience in Algeria; Portugal has not yet realized that the imperial era has come to aʳ end.

It is proper to ask here whether American nationalism has to do only with proper respect for one's own country, or with support of a military and economic imperialism that extends its greedy fingers into many parts of the developed and undeveloped world. A virtuous nationalism is one thing, a wicked imperialism is quite another.

* * *

In the third place, we might ask ourselves whether our nationalism has reference to an administration or to an aggression. We are taught as Christians to believe that government is of God. It is his will that there be order in society. It makes common sense for a people in a given geographic area to work together for the total common good.

But the institutions man creates for his service often become his masters. And thus it has frequently happened that the administration of government, the bureaucracies, the whole political apparatus becomes a master rather than a servant, seeking its own ends. Administration becomes an aggression against its people. History has thousands of examples of governments becoming aggressors, first against their own people, suppressing them, taxing them, forcing them, manipulating them, and ultimately against peoples on the outside as well.

When we have nationalistic sentiments, are we supporting an administration or have we actually already become part of the aggression? It is a question that must be asked with respect to the police forces and every part of that which was intended to be the administration of a better society.

A nationalism that has begun to police all its citizens and also tried to be a policeman of the world has gone far beyond what God intended by the institution of lawful authority.

*   *   *

Another question which might be asked is: Is nationalism a request for loyalty or is it the occasion for idolatry? The differentiation between loyalty and idolatry by the early Christians seems to be quite clear. They were prepared to obey Caesar, but they were not prepared to idolize him. They were prepared to serve but not to worship.

The Anabaptists also differentiated. This was one reason they refused to swear an oath, for swearing an oath had the implication of recognizing the rulers as divine and their authority as equal to that of God. This is also why the Mennonite, Quaker, and Brethren churches for many years discouraged their members from saluting the flag and why so many of their churches have refused to place the national flag in their sanctuaries.

I suppose that we in America and Canada would be quick to assume that nationalism obviously speaks only of loyalty but not of idolatry, but perhaps we have already been blinded and we need to take another look.

*   *   *

As a fifth test we might ask ourselves whether our nationalism has become for us truth or a source of deception. We have already reached the stage of idolatry if our loyalty or appreciation has become so intense that we are no longer able to see the sins of our society and its weaknesses in an objective light.

In this connection I would like to take a second look at some common myths evangelicals cherish regarding America.

The first is that America has always opened her doors to the distressed and persecuted. This is hardly true in the twentieth century. The Quota Act, which came into force in 1924 and which was preceded by other quota restrictions, has been operative most of this century and has kept out hundreds of thousands of people who wanted to make America their home, including many who became emigrés of the Bolshevik revolution. It also kept out the Jews trying to flee Nazi Germany, and it would have kept out Cubans, Hungarians, and Czechoslovakians if overwhelming political considerations would not have made their entry to America desirable.

A second myth is that America is the most generous nation in history. How often do we consider the extent to which America's wealth is drawn from the rest of the world, from cheap labor and unfair investment arrangements in Africa, Asia, and Latin America. When one thinks about the extent to which the American society is burning up the world's resources and energies, quite out of proportion to her ownership of these resources and quite out of proportion to her own population, one is obliged to interpret America's "generosity" somewhat differently.

A third belief is that America has never used her tremendous power to take over nations. It is true that takeovers today do not follow the pattern of former imperial takeovers, but none of the national societies whose economies are dominated by the American economy and who are overshadowed by the American military presence can accept the idea that there has been no takeover. In any event, it is not for the colonizers to say whether or not they have taken people over, but for the colonized and subjugated. They know that they have been taken over.

When Christians lose their capacity to call a nation to repentance in its most wicked moments because deception has taken the place of truth, then surely loyalty has been replaced by idolatry.

* * *

Even as we talk about nationalism as loyalty, we need to ask whether we are talking about conditional or unconditional obedience.

For the peace churches—and they believe for the early Christians as well—obedience was conditional. Whenever they felt that government was making demands in conflict with the requirements of faith, they chose not to obey; and they went to prison and to the stake for their conviction. So that we do not become too worried immediately by the suggestion that there be a selective obedience, let us recall that such is operative everywhere in our society. In Canada the government disobeyed one of its own statutes regarding wheat payments, in the hope that it could get a new statute passed before long. Many of the best lawyers in the USA believe that several presidents usurped the Constitution in the matter of the Vietnam war.

Much selective obedience is selfishness and sin, but there is also a selective obedience that is virtuous and according to the will of God. The clear principle of the New Testament that we must obey God rather than men still needs to be emphasized today, although it is clear that those who emphasize it must be prepared to pay the price, because the state itself does not recognize that principle, even when it says it is a nation under God.

* * *

Finally, we need to ask whether our nationalism represents a kingdom of this world or the kingdom of our Christ. This is another way of saying some of the things we have said before. As already indicated, nationalism can be an instrument of justice, righteousness, peace, and fulfilment for people and to that extent it is after the will of God. But, to the extent that it is against God, it is not of his kingdom.

All the kingdoms of this world are intended to become the kingdom of our Christ, but none of them *has* yet fully arrived. We need to take this into consideration, especially when we are so much tempted to think that American nationalism can be equated with the kingdom of God.

XI

A Dialogue Between Pacifists and Nonpacifists

> *"You must not think that I have come to bring peace to the earth; I have not come to bring peace but a sword."* —Matthew 10:34

> *Jesus said to him, "Put up your sword. All who take the sword die by the sword."*—Matthew 26:52

For everything its season,
and for every activity under heaven its time:
    a time to be born and a time to die. . . .
    a time to kill and a time to heal. . . .
    a time to embrace and a time to refrain from embracing. . . .
    a time to tear and a time to mend;
    a time for silence and a time for speech;
    a time to love and a time to hate;
    a time for war and a time for peace (Ecclesiastes 3:1-8).

If the preacher were writing his wisdom today, he might add that there is a time for polarization and showdown and a time for dialogue and reconciliation. No doubt there are various opinions as to which is the desired approach at what time, not least because the two are not necessarily mutually exclusive and can sometimes be a part of each other. In this essay, at any rate, we shall place the emphasis on dialogue.

We have chosen dialogue for reasons of principle. In any one situation it should be our concern to give the full truth and new insights a maximum opportunity. In the present circumstances, it seems to me, more truth can emerge from sympathetic and open conversation than through a dogged and uncompromising confrontation.

The mass media have in recent years given mass dimensions to man's tendency to look at life and his fellow beings in terms of stereotypes. In our time this means classifying the events, movements, organizations, people, and issues in certain well-defined categories, giving them labels, and viewing them as either wholly good or wholly bad. Our list of categories and labels is almost endless. We divide life, events, people, issues into

> pacifism—militarism,
> Communist—non-Communist,
> left—right,
> Christian—non-Christian,
> Catholic—Protestant,
> East—West,
> evangelical—liberal,
> white—nonwhite,
> protesters—establishment.

Instead of examining each new phenomenon critically for the good or evil it may contain in itself, we resolve the matter by associating it with one of the categories or stereotypes, which we have already labelled good or bad. When we do this, truth always suffers.

There is no need to reject the protesters, or the establishment for that matter, in everything they say and do just because there are some things they say or do that we disapprove. Similarly, our appreciation of Western society does not mean that we must accept all of it uncritically or reject Eastern society wholesale—or vice versa. Let us learn to accept truth and good wherever it may be found and reject untruth and evil in whatever form it may appear.

There may, indeed, be a time for sharper confrontation, but for the time being too much can be gained from an all-sided conversation for us to bypass this method of discovering truth. Let us proceed then to lay a foundation for our dialogue.

* * *

First of all, let us admit that the literature and theology

of the sacred books is somewhat ambivalent on the question before us. The two Scripture passages at the head of this essay, both sayings of Jesus recorded in the Book of Matthew, seem to contradict each other. In one instance, the Lord predicts the sword as an inevitable by-product, perhaps even one ingredient, of discipleship; in the second he appears to deny the use of the sword to his disciples.

There are other apparent contradictions in Jesus' life as it is reviewed in the Gospels. On the one hand, we see him forcefully uprooting the profiteers in the temple (Matthew 21:12-13), and on the other hand we hear him objecting to the use of fire from heaven for hostile villagers (Luke 9:51-56). His apostle successors can likewise be quoted to support either view. Paul's words in Romans 13 have been used to exalt the authority of the state as normative for Christians; while the insistence of Peter and John that believers should obey God rather than men (Acts 5:29) has been used to deny such status to the state.

The role of the state in the life of the believer has throughout church history been a most difficult one. Even if we could agree that the writings of the New Testament resolve this question in favor of pacifism, there is still the Old Testament, also part of the biblical canon, to be dealt with. And very few theologians, if any, have resolved the contradictions therein to the satisfaction of any sizeable number of Christians. Similar problems are presented by the sacred writings of other religions, the Koran for instance. While the Prophet Muhammad has a great deal to say about *jihad* or holy war, he is not the complete warrior he has often been made out to be in the West.

Admittedly, what one reads out of the sacred writings depends a great deal on one's approach. A good case can be made for an entirely new reading of the Bible, but that new approach too must be part of the dialogue. For the moment we can acknowledge that, when both sides approach the Bible as a flat book and extract from its contents proof-texts to support a particular point of view, as both pacifists and nonpacifists have frequently done, one does end up with theological support for both sides of the issue.

* * *

Secondly, we can acknowledge that both pacifists and nonpacifists claim to be pursuing the same goal, namely peace for mankind. Each side is usually suspicious of the other side's methods, however. The one side says that peace is not, cannot be, the fruit of war, while the other side says that the pursuit of peace sometimes makes war necessary, and what is necessary is acceptable if not desirable. US Civil War hero and President Ulysses S. Grant once said, "I have never advocated war except as a means of peace."

The same argument led to the entry of the USA and other nations into the two world wars. Both were wars to end all wars and to make the world safe for peace and democracy. It would be difficult indeed to find anyone associated with a defense establishment who would not admit to aspirations for peace. The bombers of the Strategic Air Command, for example, are always flying "peace missions."

One may say that in all this talk about peace there is much insincerity and hypocrisy, and that one cannot and should not take all the nice verbalisms seriously; that men are known by their fruits; that it is impossible to separate ends from means; and that an announced goal has to be evaluated in terms of the method chosen to attain it. It is good to point to possible contradictions between words and deeds and between ends and means. But in each case we can offer the benefit of our doubt and conclude that the problem of our dialogue is not first of all the formulation of similar goals but rather the determination of the right and adequate means.

* * *

Thirdly, we would do well to recognize that both pacifists and militarists, seen in absolute terms either in theory or practice, are very hard to find.

Each side sees the other in black and white terms, although pacifists have probably been guilty of the greatest distortions in viewing both themselves and their opposites.

Many militarists have more pacifism in them than either they or pacifists have been ready to admit, and many pacifists have more military potential in them than they

125

have been willing to recognize. As social psychologist John Elias said recently, noting strong aggressive and violent tendencies among members of the so-called "peace churches": "Under certain conditions almost everybody will be cruel to his fellowman." It is not at all uncommon for those who condemn war to express themselves in favor of the violent overthrow of the establishment. They may condemn the just war but advocate a just revolution, violence and all.

Similarly, most of the militarists have begun to espouse a degree of pacifism. To them violence in the streets is very bad and silly little wars between infantile little nations or tribes (Nigeria and Biafra, or Honduras and El Salvador) are foolish indeed. Sometimes it appears that in the eyes of the big-nation militarists, all the little wars are no good and that, in the eyes of little-nation militarists, all the big-power conflicts are bad.

The pacifists and the militarists have much in common, because, generally speaking, they are not as far to the opposite ends of the scale as both believe. They can both be found somewhere along a continuum. We are confronted, therefore, not completely by differences in kind but rather by differences of degree, and to acknowledge this would give us a new basis for dialogue. All of us are in part militarist and part pacifist. We should start our dialogue with that assumption.

*   *   *

In the fourth place, both pacifists and nonpacifists have major sins of omission. These sins are not the same, or even of the same kind, but they are both major sins in the context of the respective positions.

Pacifism in history has very often been a passivity that shirked involvement and responsibility. Some conscientious objectors, for instance, are clearly escapists; and many conscientious objectors have been opposed to war on personal grounds only and could readily accept others fighting for them, as though they were too Christian to do it themselves.

An even greater neglect is that pacifists have generally failed to give much attention to alternate strategies of conflict resolution. (Some Quakers represent a strong ex-

126

ception here.) In defense of pacifists one might say that society itself has been emotionally and financially uncooperative in working out alternatives to armed conflict, but this does not excuse them entirely. It remains true that there has been very little social and political follow-through on their theoretical position by the pacifists.

Militarists, on the other hand, are singularly remiss in public self-criticism and have failed to examine sufficiently their own positions. They almost give the impression that militarism cannot stand examination. If the pacifists have failed to be logical and consequential in their follow-through, the nonpacifists who hold to the just war theory have as often fallen down in examining their own positions. More often than not they have accepted their countries' wars without ever bothering to ask whether they were just.

Both pacifists and nonpacifists have manifested so many weaknesses in the context of their own positions that both have reasons to be humble and to engage in dialogue together, for they both need each other to overcome their respective problems.

*　　*　　*

Finally, both pacifists and nonpacifists are confronted by the common agenda of our violent humanity and what to do about our armed society. Neither can be happy about recent developments in North American society; namely, increased dependence on arms on the part of the police in restoring law and order and increased dependence on arms on the part of the people for their security. We are rapidly becoming a domestic society armed to the teeth, and the end result cannot be a happy one for anyone.

We are arming ourselves physically, of course, because we are already armed psychologically. Our society is filled with hostility and fear. Its members are at war within themselves and with each other. Where there is psychological war, it is only a question of time before there is physical war. Unless the process of psychological and physical disarmament begins soon, miniature civil wars (we will call them increases in crime) will break out all over our nations, and both of us, pacifists and nonpacifists, will

127

wish that something could be done to reduce the level of hostility and the use of arms.

The time to begin is now, and we do not first have to establish where we all stand on the pacifist-militarist continuum before we can get on with the job. All of us must increase confidence, trust, and fearlessness, and all of us must seek means other than clubs and guns to achieve neighborhood tranquility. It is impossible to think of a community, large or small, being at peace at the point of a gun.

Today all the world has become a neighborhood and it is proper to speak of the entire world as a domestic situation. What is true about psychological and physical warfare and disarmament within nations is true also among nations. And, whether pacifist or nonpacifist, all of us must be very deeply concerned when we hear our generals glorying in the vision of a battlefield on which we can destroy anything we locate through instant communications by almost instantaneous application of highly lethal firepower.

Whatever our position, society has laid out before us a common agenda, and in the final analysis we will not be asked how we defined our position but what we did about the problems confronting us.